ADVANCE PRAISE FOR
THE LEADERSHIP EQUATION

"What builds great organizations? Eric Douglas has gifted us all with the answer and the roadmap in *The Leadership Equation*. Implement his principles and you'll find yourself the leader of a powerful, hyper-creative, high-achieving organizational culture!"

—Marshall Goldsmith, author of the *New York Times* and global bestseller *What Got You Here Won't Get You There*

"This is a great book and a great read. It describes what moves us at our core as human beings and how to inspire leadership throughout an organization."

—Anne Stausboll, CEO, CalPERS

"In successful companies, trust and innovation go hand in hand . . . When they coexist, an organization's capacity for success grows exponentially. *The Leadership Equation* hits you with a one-two punch; Eric helps you engender trust among your team even as you spark their innovative drive. As he demonstrates, when you can do both, you create a leadership culture that helps the whole organization excel."

—Judith E. Glaser, author of the bestseller *Conversational Intelligence: How Great Leaders Build Trust and Get Extraordinary Results*; CEO of Benchmark Communications; and chairman of The Creating WE Institute

"Eric Douglas couldn't be clearer: spark plus trust is a winning formula for leaders and their organizations. These ten practices ring true and, more importantly, are actionable. By taking these simple, proactive steps, you can boost creativity and collaboration, empower employees to make the best choices for the business, and lead your team to success."

—John Baldoni, chair of the leadership development practice at N2growth; author of *MOXIE: The Secret to Bold and Gutsy Leadership* and *Lead with Purpose*

"The fast pace and constant change of today's business environment present challenges to any organization, large or small. Douglas provides a roadmap for structuring an organization to flourish in this environment. *The Leadership Equation* is an essential read for any leader intent on building a high-performing organization."

—Marty McGartland, President and CEO of Natoma Technologies

"I heartily recommend this well-written, wise book on successful leadership and innovation. It will be an invaluable guide to anyone who is in a position of leadership or who aspires to lead."

—Dr. Robert L. Hendren, professor and vice chair of psychiatry, University of California, San Francisco

THE
LEADERSHIP EQUATION

THE

LEADERSHIP EQUATION

10 Practices That Build Trust,
Spark Innovation, and
Create High-Performing Organizations

ERIC DOUGLAS

GREENLEAF
BOOK GROUP PRESS

Published by Greenleaf Book Group Press
Austin, Texas
www.gbgpress.com

Distributed by Greenleaf Book Group

For ordering information or special discounts for bulk purchases, please contact Greenleaf Book Group at PO Box 91869, Austin, TX 78709, 512.891.6100.

Design and composition by Greenleaf Book Group
Cover design by Greenleaf Book Group
Cover imagery: © iStockphoto / bowie15

Cataloging-in-Publication data

Douglas, Eric, 1950-
  The leadership equation : 10 practices that build trust, spark innovation, and create high performing organizations / Eric Douglas.—First edition.
     pages : illustrations ; cm
  Issued also as an ebook.
  Includes bibliographical references and index.
  ISBN: 978-1-62634-088-6
  1. Leadership. 2. Personnel management. 3. Trust. 4. Employee motivation.
5. Success in business. I. Title.
HD57.7 .D68 2014
658.4/092   2014939725

Part of the Tree Neutral® program, which offsets the number of trees consumed in the production and printing of this book by taking proactive steps, such as planting trees in direct proportion to the number of trees used: www.treeneutral.com

TreeNeutral®

Printed in the United States of America on acid-free paper

14 15 16 17 18 19   10 9 8 7 6 5 4 3 2 1

First Edition

FOR MY PARENTS, PETER AND ALICE

CONTENTS

PREFACE

My firm specializes in change. It's a good business to be in, given today's fast-moving world. Our team of consultants provides leaders and managers with the specific skill sets and frameworks that facilitate change and build successful organizations. For example, in the past few years, we helped the leaders of a Los Angeles nonprofit develop a sustainable system to educate more than three hundred thousand inner-city youth. We helped the leaders of a $9 billion state agency transform itself from a slow-moving bureaucracy into a highly focused organization that other states are trying to emulate. We helped a California-based medical group figure out how to improve care for more than fifty thousand patients, saving lives and millions of dollars.

In the course of our work, we frequently meet leaders who are frustrated by the barrage of management advice they receive. People like:

- The CEO of a Boston hospital: "I was trained first and foremost as a doctor. Now I manage five thousand people. Things are happening so fast. I don't know if I'm thinking the right way or doing the right things."

- The COO of a technology start-up: "How do I build a successful culture? Where do I focus? On training the frontline staff? On serving customers? On planning? What's the right balance?"

- The director of a nonprofit: "All I do is respond to questions and put out fires all day. Did business school teach me how to lead in this kind of environment? Well, we attended a three-day leadership seminar. But the short answer is no!"

These people, and thousands more like them, want practical tools to guide them. Over the past fifteen years, our firm has paid close attention to the practices that build great organizations. The result is this book, *The Leadership Equation*. As you'll learn, the leadership equation taps deeply into what motivates us as human beings. Thus it is both familiar and surprising at the same time. The leadership equation can help you focus on the practices that will improve the performance of your team, your business unit, and your entire organization. It will help you coach the people around you. Ultimately, it will help you reach your full potential as a leader.

I trust that *The Leadership Equation* will prove valuable to you. In exchange, I have a request: please share what helps you be an effective leader. What special techniques have you learned? What challenges do you face? Go to our website, www.leadingresources.com, and click on the Leadership Equation icon. There you can share your thoughts directly with me.

In closing, let me cite Mark Twain: "Keep away from people who try to belittle your ambitions. Small people always do that, but the really great make you feel that you, too, can become great."

ACKNOWLEDGMENTS

Many people helped me in the writing of this book. First, my colleagues and the extraordinary consultants at Leading Resources Inc., where we are working every day to develop leaders and leading organizations. Thanks especially to Karin Bloomer, Marcia Tennyson, and Robert Emerson for being with me on this journey and providing input for this book. I also want to tip my hat to our amazing support team: thank you Lauren, Leslie, Aaron, and Matt.

I want to thank our clients. Many of you will recognize yourselves in the chapters of this book. It is an honor to earn your trust and to work with you.

I want to thank the people at Greenleaf Book Group. Their team helped me fine tune this book and bring it to the market looking its best.

I want to acknowledge many friends for their insights and their trust in me. A special thank-you goes to John Webre, Sydney Coatsworth, Margaret Kane, Tom Paine, and Shaw Warren. To my sister, Penelope, thank you for your love and insights over the years. Last, I want to thank my family. First, my wife, Susanna, with whom I enjoy the greatest journey of all. To my four children, Kate, Charlotte, Abigail, and James: you teach me lessons in leadership each day. As of this writing, my three young grandchildren also deserve mention: Alex, Sam, and Alice. I also want to acknowledge and thank my parents, Peter and Alice, for giving me the education and inspiration to do what I do.

INTRODUCTION

I had a dream while I was working on this book. In the dream, I was speaking to a group of leaders about the practices that build high-performing organizations. A cluster of people gathered around me, asking me questions. One person said: "Don't you have a simple formula?"

At that time I didn't have a formula or a Grand Unified Theory. But in my dream, I turned to a convenient white board (dreams are handy that way) and wrote down this equation:

$$T \text{ (TRUST)} + S \text{ (SPARK)} = LC \text{ (LEADERSHIP CULTURE)}$$

I awoke from my dream and went into the kitchen to write the formula down. And in the days following my dream, I thought about it more. And I realized that all the different practices that go into making a great company fit under the formula of $T + S = LC$. The equation captures profoundly—and at the same time, simply—a framework for understanding the fundamental things that effective leaders do to build a "leadership culture"—in which everyone runs it like they own it.

They focus on building trust, and they focus on generating innovation (spark).

One of my best friends, John, is an architect. We think about things in similar ways. When he designs a building, he thinks about its organic fit within its site, about the light at different times of day. He focuses on the building's strength, durability, and sustainability. He thinks about how people will live in the building, the flow, the communication from room to room, from floor to floor. And he thinks about the costs and the benefits of different designs.

In our firm, we think of ourselves as architects of organizations. We work with corporations, nonprofits, public agencies, cooperatives, and many other kinds of organizations to achieve the same things: strength, sustainability, and coherency of structure. Communication and flow. The agility of the company to respond to challenges. And (of course) revenues, costs, and profits.

But regardless of the kind of organization, we've learned there are ten specific practices that leaders must put into play to make an organization great. Five fit under the T side of the equation. Five fit under S. The equation provides the mental model, the framework. The specific practices make the model come to life.

WHY TRUST AND SPARK?

Most people don't immediately think of trust and spark when they think about great companies. They think about products (GE), or services (Fidelity). They think about brands (Apple). They think about iconic CEOs and strong growth. But most people haven't had the opportunity to peer under the hoods of dozens of organizations to see what makes them run smoothly. Or to recognize what's common to them all.

Our firm has had the honor and privilege to get under the hood and work with many great (and a few not-so-great) companies and organizations. In our role as consultants and coaches to CEOs and organizations around the globe, we're able to see up close the day-to-day behaviors of people in charge of running and building companies. We've been given the opportunity to try different strategies. And we see what works.

So what have we observed? First, the best-performing companies and organizations invest in building cultures where talented people come to work each day not dreading what they do but truly believing in the company and its products and services and eager to add value. These are cultures where people are inculcated with the spirit of stewardship, of running it like they own it. Where people know that they can disagree, hash it out, and come together as one to focus on getting something done.

Second, we've observed that communication is the glue that builds great companies. Communication is the real currency—not money—because communication builds trust. As Lou Gerstner, the former CEO of IBM, once said: "It's about communication. It's about honesty. It's about treating people in the organization as deserving to know the facts. You don't try to give them half the story. You don't try to hide the story. You treat them as true equals, and you communicate and you communicate and communicate." People need to trust one another if they're going to work together effectively. They need to regularly engage in tough conversations,[1] identifying issues, chewing on options, figuring out the best approach, and going into battle thinking as one. Without trust, people will quickly resort to their own selfish behaviors, sowing discord and eventually wreaking havoc in the company.

Third, we've observed that great companies—particularly as the pace of change accelerates—are fired up to innovate. Innovation happens because people feel free to envision new products, services, and ways of doing things. It happens because people trust that their ideas will be received positively. They can envision a future in which their creativity will yield something better—both for the company and for themselves.

Now, the currency of innovation is different from the currency of trust. Whereas communication builds trust, empowerment generates spark. People need to feel empowered—that they literally have the power—to experiment and try things. This means creating pockets of local invention, where small teams work together unburdened by bureaucratic oversight. Tightly knit teams are not necessarily the most creative. Loosely structured teams, with a clear goal but without domineering presences, can give people the room to think before they share results with the group.

Envision an engine room with two levers on the floor. Pull one and you generate high levels of trust. People share responsibility, cooperate readily, and accept compromises swiftly. Pull the other and you stoke the fires of innovation. People quickly identify gaps in quality and fill them, and eagerly sponge up new ideas and put them to work building value. Pull both levers together, and you have a leadership culture. What's important is that you understand the dynamics of these two forces: trust and spark. That's what we'll look at next.

THE ORIGINS OF TRUST

To understand how fundamental trust truly is, we have to go back to the beginning. As it turns out, we humans are hardwired to seek situations in which we feel trust, because our brains release high levels of oxytocin when we experience trust.[2] Oxytocin is a neurotransmitter that makes us feel good and gives us positive feelings about the people around us. As a result, we are able to work through our disagreements and not harbor grudges. We cooperate in extraordinary ways.

Every one of our emotions stems from our feelings of trust—or the lack of it. On the positive side, trust gives rise to feelings of generosity, joy, courage, empowerment, self-confidence, tenderness, intimacy, and love. On the negative side, a lack of trust gives rise to feelings of anger, betrayal, jealousy, resentment, and vengefulness—and worse. Why do we feel love? Because we trust someone to look after our interests, and we feel trusted in return. Why do we feel betrayed? Because we perceive someone isn't keeping up his end of the bargain. Why do we feel jealous? Because someone else is getting the deal we think we deserved to get.

Trust is based on the principle of predictable returns. If I do this for you, I'll get this in return. The shorthand term is "reciprocity." In his book *How the Mind Works*,[3] Steven Pinker shows exactly how our brains are wired to respond to actions that build trust. He points out that reciprocity is an evolutionary strategy, hardwired into our genes. If you give me a hand, I'll return the favor—especially if I think there's a strong likelihood of repeated transactions with you in the future. Trust hinges on having enough information over time to determine whether reciprocity occurs. Pinker shows that our brains are hardwired to detect whether reciprocity and trust exist—or whether we're getting the short end of the stick. This "cheater meter" is working in every conscious moment. If I think that you've treated me fairly, in ways that I predicted, then my cheater meter is in the green. If not, it swings into the red.

You may not know it, but our cheater meters are working all the time. When we feel trust, our cheater meter fades into the background. Everything feels good (that's the oxytocin talking). But our cheater meters emerge the moment we experience distrust. Did your boss not include you in a decision that affects you? Did your peer forget to inform you about a meeting with one of your employees? Think about it. You know vividly when you distrust someone. Your cheater meter is a finely tuned instrument—one that you may not have even known existed. It's working right now as you read this book. Do you feel you're getting useful information? Is this what you hoped to be learning? That's your cheater meter at work.

Let's add another layer of nuance to this trust business: Each of us sets our cheater meter a bit differently. This is particularly evident at the start of a relationship. Some people trust until they have data that convinces them otherwise. Some people distrust until they see evidence that they can trust. And a small percentage are on the margins: they either trust too much or rarely feel trust. Look at the following table and think about where your cheater meter is set.

TRUST STILL	TRUST UNTIL	DISTRUST UNTIL	DISTRUST STILL
I almost always trust people.	I trust people until I see evidence that I shouldn't.	I don't trust people until I see evidence that I should.	I rarely trust people.

If you said "trust until," you join roughly 45 percent of the population who feel that way. Another 45 percent say they "distrust until." The remaining 10 percent occupy the two extremes, again in roughly even percentages. People have different trust orientations. That's important to remember as you think about strategies for building trust.

Another dimension of trust has to do with expectations. Some people have very high expectations and thus are easily disappointed. Others have low expectations, and don't feel particularly bothered when their expectations aren't met.

BUILDING TRUST

So how do you build trust? Well, that's the subject of this entire book. At the most basic level, trust is about reciprocity. Reciprocity means getting treated fairly. In a work setting, this means people feel trust when they are paid fairly for the work they do. They feel trust when they are recognized for a job well done. Reciprocity hinges on predictability. If you've said something will occur if certain expectations are met, you'd better adhere to the deal—otherwise you'll set off a chain reaction of distrust.

Trust is not just about reciprocity. It's about speed. In a world where information flows at the speed of light, the speed of trust is the speed at which a colleague voluntarily communicates information that is important for you to know. For example, if I have the inside scoop on a competitor's new marketing push, the speed of trust is reflected in how quickly I send you that information.

Trust obviously depends on communication. Trust means that every employee, starting at the top, knows the organization's goals. Trust means that roles and responsibilities are clear, and that the rules for dealing with conflicts are well understood. Trust means holding people accountable for what they do and don't do. High levels of trust enable people to listen to each other's views, to talk about tough issues, to share information, and to work together as a team.

Another important element of trust is transparency—letting people know what's going on even if the news is not all good. W. L. Gore, the maker of Gore-Tex fabric, provides regular updates to every employee on how the company is doing in meeting its goals. Senior management goes out of its way to communicate what's going on with revenues and profits. Among mid-sized companies, it's consistently ranked number one in *Fortune* magazine's survey of best companies to work for. It's also one of the most profitable.

Transparency also builds trust with customers and shareholders. Transparent pricing is one example. Anyone who bought a car in the twentieth century was accustomed to dealing with an informational black hole. In the twenty-first century, auto dealers build trust with their customers by being open about their pricing and profits—and the experience is infinitely better. eBay builds trust by showing where your bid stands in relation to others and providing tips on how to place the winning bid. Google builds trust by sharing detailed compensation information. Transparency builds trust.

Perhaps the highest form of trust building is reciprocal communication. Reciprocal communication means you treat people around you

FOUR COMPETENCIES THAT BUILD TRUST

....

When employees feel high levels of trust, they feel a sense of calm happiness. They take pride in their work, they communicate openly and honestly, and to the extent they can, they think of themselves as stewards, running the business like they own it. A lack of trust breeds the opposite feeling. It causes people to draw inward, to not communicate openly, to feel resentful, and ultimately to do the bare minimum to get by.

Leaders and managers inspire trust via the competencies they display. Consider the following:

Trust in vision: Employees trust that the company's leaders have a grasp on trends in the marketplace and are positioning the company to capitalize on those trends, even if it means wrenching change in the current business. This is the kind of trust that prevailed at Apple when Steve Jobs was CEO.

Trust in operations: Employees trust that leaders are effective in managing the business and keeping it well organized. They see the company is achieving its business goals and objectives, that people and teams mesh together well, and that people understand what's expected of them. This is the kind of trust that prevails at Southwest Airlines.

Trust in communication: Employees trust that they're being kept abreast of important news about goals, programs, policies, and people. People trust their leaders are informing them right away about new hires, people leaving, or people being promoted. In general there are no surprises because management communicates effectively.

Trust in professional development: Employees trust that their own professional development is being tended to, that their bosses are taking time to mentor them, to give them honest feedback about what they're doing well and to identify specific areas for improvement. Employees are encouraged to take advantage of training opportunities and rewarded when they do so.

A lack of any of these four competencies affects how people feel about the organization. When trust in vision is lacking, for example, employees feel

(continued)

nervous about the business's long-term future. They question whether management understands what's happening or is responding appropriately. The more talented people will begin to leave. In the worst circumstances, there is a stampede for the door.

When trust in operations is lacking, employees feel frustrated by the time and energy they waste. They lose energy to suggest improvements and resign themselves to the status quo. In the worst cases, employees ridicule management while managers harangue them to improve.

When trust in communications is lacking, employees rely on informal channels to learn what's going on. Gossip prevails. People feel less willing to contribute or communicate proactively. Over time, employees become suspicious about what management is trying to hide and—in the worst cases—openly defy management.

When trust in professional development is lacking, employees feel less loyal to their managers. They feel less inclined to work hard or sacrifice their personal time for training. Morale declines. In the worst cases, employees no longer feel committed to high standards of performance.

A lack of trust in any of these four dimensions will cause the company's performance to erode. The solution is to give the CEO and other senior leaders the coaching they need to display these competencies and get other managers to follow their lead—and by doing so restore trust.

as equals—valuing their ideas and showing visibly that you respect their views, even if their ideas are different from your own. As a leader, you should convene people regularly so that they can identify hot issues, share views, debate approaches, and agree on a common course of action. The CEO of a large utility company, one of our clients, convenes his executive team for an all-day meeting every six weeks so that the team can grapple with emerging issues and challenges, discuss options, and decide together what to do. The company is recognized as one of the best-run businesses in the industry.

THE ORIGINS OF SPARK

Trust is the key, but it's not the whole picture. Spark is the second part of the equation. Spark occurs when people's creative energies are flowing.

Spark means providing people with the freedom to explore new ideas without fear. Spark means people feel deeply engaged in devising ways to improve the business. Spark happens when there's a big vision, clearly communicated, and the entire team is focused on achieving that vision. It exists when there are clear performance measures tied to the things that matter and performance is evaluated fairly and consistently.

Spark is related to the idea of "flow"—first introduced by the social psychologist Mihaly Csikszentmihalyi. In great organizations, trust and spark feed off one another. Trust sets the stage for productive innovation (i.e., innovation that is in service to the goals of the organization). When you build trust, people become open to change. By energizing employees with spark, you unleash the innovation that makes an organization vibrate with new ideas and real purpose. Together, trust and spark create a culture in which people feel deeply engaged and committed to the company's success.

3M is a good example of a company that focuses on trust and spark. Its "15 percent rule" enables employees to spend 15 percent of their work time exploring and conducting experiments. Technical employees can apply for internal corporate grants to fund innovative projects they want to pursue. It's this careful nurturing of innovation that has resulted in products like ScotchGard™ and Thinsulate™. Giving employees a day each week to innovate as they choose is a practice at many leading companies, including Facebook, Twitter, and Google.

Fred Smith, the founder and CEO of Federal Express, has a similar strategy for his company: "We hammer home that *not to change* is to be in the process of dying, of not meeting the market as it is. We applaud people who instigate change. We don't hang people who try something new that doesn't work out, because that's the easiest way to ossify an organization—to crucify the people who are trying to innovate."[4]

BUILDING SPARK

By now, everyone is familiar with the story of how the two Steves—Wozniak and Jobs—pretty much created the personal computer industry. Steve Jobs put a premium on fun, creativity, learning, and exploring new ideas: "Learning about new technologies and markets is what makes this fun for me," Jobs was fond of saying. "You just got to go learn this stuff. If you're smart, you'll figure it out."[5]

Spark thrives in an environment of freedom, where the unexpected is invited, embraced, and encouraged to evolve into value. Walt Disney understood it. Long before Mickey Mouse came along, he injected creativity into his team of animators. He wasn't content to have silent cartoons: he wanted the first cartoons with sound. He wasn't content with black and white: he wanted color. The people who worked with Disney often remarked on the freedom he gave them to try new things—and they drew on the culture he built to come up with their own dazzling creations.

Here's a story about Walt's ingenuity. In 1934, while making his masterpiece of animation, *Snow White and the Seven Dwarfs*, Disney became dissatisfied with the limitations of two-dimensional backgrounds. He wanted to convey depth realistically, yet all he had to work with was animation cells on photographic plates. So Disney challenged his team to find a better way.

The result was the multiplane camera, an elaborate, one-story-tall device with a dozen moving glass panels on which his animators could superimpose different backdrops. By subtly shifting the positions of the glass panels with each shot, Disney's animators successfully conveyed the illusion of three dimensions in *Snow White*.[6] Remember, this is 1937!

Through his constant quest for creative quality, Disney sparked his teams of animators and producers to think freely and create great things. Walt Disney Studios innovated, learned from its mistakes, and blossomed into one of the most successful companies in the world.

Spark isn't limited to the private sector. Ted Gaebler, coauthor of *Reinventing Government*,[7] sees innovation as one of government's most important missions: "We need to start engaging public employees' whole brains," he says, "not just the expenditure control half. We need to engage the entrepreneurial brain as well."

It's easy to spot companies with high levels of spark:

- People feel free to challenge the status quo.
- People go way beyond what you normally expect.
- People feel their work is fun.
- People feel unconstrained by rank or hierarchy to suggest improvements.
- People aren't afraid to share their ideas about how to improve things.

One of the best examples of spark is Google. Here's a company that a decade or so ago barely registered a ripple. Today, its innovations influence everything from advertising and media to geoscience, disease control, and climate prediction. In the next several years, Google's innovations will enable your refrigerator to communicate your shopping list directly to the grocery store, guide your car as it navigates down the highway, and convert your home into a mini-generating plant. Google has created a new kind of company, one that blends the best of a nonprofit with the best of a for-profit. By operating with high levels of spark, it has rearranged and reshaped everything we do.

THE LEADERSHIP EQUATION

Once I realized the basic formula $(T + S = LC)$, the next step was to expand it to include the specific practices that build trust and generate spark. This resulted in the expanded leadership equation—or the Grand Theory of Organizational Excellence. Notice that there are ten practices, corresponding to the ten chapters of this book. Five of the practices build trust and five create spark.

TRUST	SPARK
Align the Core Values (ACV)	Accelerate the Pace of Change (APC)
Sharpen the Focus (STF)	Stimulate Creative Flow (SCF)
Lead Through Others (LTO)	Spread Systems Thinking (SST)
Manage Decisions Well (MDW)	Multiply the Communication (MTC)
Start With Yourself (SWY)	Ask Powerful Questions (APQ)

Using these acronyms, the expanded equation looks like this:

$$(ACV+STF+LTO+MDW+SWY) + (APC+SCF+SST+MTC+APQ) = LC$$

Though the practices are divided into two groups, trust and spark are not separate engines. As mentioned earlier, they are more like a combined cycle power plant in which trust fuels innovation and innovation generates trust. They work synergistically, and all ten need to be employed to build a leadership culture.

Let me reiterate why this is: Human beings are hardwired to respond positively to trust and spark. Neither on its own is enough. In cultures that are high in trust but low in spark, people feel respect and trust for one another, but their creative energies are not engaged in continuously improving the enterprise. In cultures that are high in spark but low in trust, people behave entrepreneurially but fail to make their ideas mesh, so conflict abounds.

IMPACT ON CULTURE

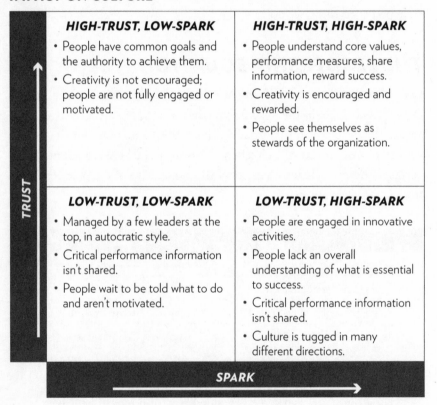

TRUST	**HIGH-TRUST, LOW-SPARK**	**HIGH-TRUST, HIGH-SPARK**
	• People have common goals and the authority to achieve them.	• People understand core values, performance measures, share information, reward success.
	• Creativity is not encouraged; people are not fully engaged or motivated.	• Creativity is encouraged and rewarded.
		• People see themselves as stewards of the organization.
	LOW-TRUST, LOW-SPARK	**LOW-TRUST, HIGH-SPARK**
	• Managed by a few leaders at the top, in autocratic style.	• People are engaged in innovative activities.
	• Critical performance information isn't shared.	• People lack an overall understanding of what is essential to success.
	• People wait to be told what to do and aren't motivated.	• Critical performance information isn't shared.
		• Culture is tugged in many different directions.
	SPARK	

The best organizations focus on both trust and spark. In those companies, people are consistently engaged and thinking and acting in ways that lead to the company's overall success. They attract and retain the most talented employees. They innovate constantly. They surprise and delight their customers. They outperform their peers. When trust and spark work together, people feel free, ask powerful questions, and air conflicting opinions. The culture shifts from one in which people focus on their jobs to one in which people focus on the performance of the entire organization. When you're operating with trust and spark, everyone runs it like they own it. As you'll learn in the next ten chapters, companies like Zappos, Apple, and Southwest Airlines have become phenomenally successful by following this formula for building a leadership culture.

ALIGN THE CORE VALUES

(ACV+STF+LTO+MDW+SWY) + (APC+SCF+SST+MTC+APQ) = LC

In 1986, Ken Iverson took over as CEO of Nucor, a maker of steel prod-ucts based in Kansas City.[1] He inherited a stodgy corporate culture char-acterized by hostile relationships between management and rank and file. Until Iverson, Nucor appeared destined for oblivion.

Iverson turned the culture around by doing three things:

1. He did away with titles.
2. He did away with hierarchies.
3. He did away with all executive perks. (Until that point, executive importance was determined by club memberships and access to the company's executive dining room.)

His goal was clear—he sought to eliminate the "we" versus "them" mentality that cripples organizations. Under Iverson, Nucor negotiated a highly successful profit-sharing arrangement with its trade unions. He also embraced—rather than feared—foreign competition.

With Iverson at the helm, Nucor changed its values, its structure, and its culture—and that, in turn, enabled it to achieve an extraordinary level of success. In fact, when you compare Nucor's performance to that of one of its chief competitors, Bethlehem Steel, what you see over a fifteen-year period is nothing short of amazing. Nucor increased its share value to more than twenty times that of Bethlehem Steel.[2]

Tony Hsieh, the CEO of Zappos, the shoe and clothing company, has built a phenomenally successful company by aligning employees around ten core values. Employees are hired and fired based on the ten core values. The core values are prominently displayed on Zappos' website. In fact, each box of shoes is inscribed with one of the core values. How successful is Zappos? Consider this: Starting in 1999, when Hsieh joined the company, it had virtually no sales. Ten years later, it had grown to over $1 billion in gross sales annually.

Zappos' ten core values are:

1. Deliver WOW Through Service
2. Embrace and Drive Change
3. Create Fun and a Little Weirdness
4. Be Adventurous, Creative, and Open-Minded
5. Pursue Growth and Learning
6. Build Open and Honest Relationships With Communication
7. Build a Positive Team and Family Spirit
8. Do More With Less
9. Be Passionate and Determined
10. Be Humble

So how have these ten core values created a leadership culture at Zappos? Here are three interesting innovations that the core values have sparked:

- The company provides free shipping both ways.
- Zappos has a 365-day return policy.
- Sales staffers don't have scripts.

"If you get the culture right, then most of the other stuff, like great customer service or building a brand will just happen naturally," Hsieh says. Building a leadership culture that gives employees freedom and space is the essence of what Hsieh has done to make Zappos so successful.

These two examples show what is possible when leaders engage in a deep exploration of their companies' core values and shift the culture from one that is personality driven to one that is values driven. In the process of aligning core values, underlying conflicts are forced to the surface. Tough discussions occur about what is truly essential to the enterprise. As people become aligned, they can take on more authority and responsibility. As they feel more empowered, morale and productivity increase. It's a virtuous cycle!

"We are constantly making sure people are aligned with our values," says Laura Batten, the CEO of a consumer goods manufacturing company. "It is the secret to our strong performance year after year." Her recipe includes annual surveys of all employees to assess where the organization is adhering to its core values—and where it's falling short. She follows up by facilitating employee forums to share the survey results and brainstorm ideas for improving in those areas that score low. For example, when "maintaining work-life balance" scored low, she made a public commitment to reducing overtime and backed it up with initiatives to distribute workload more evenly.

Defining the organization's core values—and applying them—is the first step in developing a leadership culture. Aligning your people around a framework of core values brings multiple benefits. It frees managers from the suffocating constraint of having to second-guess every decision and micromanage every detail. In a values-driven organization, managers can delegate decisions and ask people to think for themselves. When people act on the basis of clearly understood values—linked to performance measures—they are naturally engaged in making the right decisions consistently over time.

Alignment also attracts other talented people. It's easier to get the right people to join your organization when you can clearly communicate what's important, and what behaviors you're looking for. This reduces turnover, thereby cutting the costs associated with recruiting, retaining, and retraining employees. In a service economy with higher intrinsic labor costs and increasing labor mobility, this is an important source of competitive advantage and profit.

Focusing on core values and vision also attracts and retains loyal customers. People are attracted to companies they trust—that are value driven. Smart companies use this to build tight bonds with their customers. Zappos, Starbucks, Google, Apple, Southwest, Nordstrom, IBM, and Porsche are all examples of companies that have effectively aligned their employees and customers around a set of core values.

It always surprises me to learn that a company pays only lip service to its core values, since operating from a well-understood framework of core values can have such a positive impact. I've come to believe that many people don't really understand what core values mean—or how to identify them successfully. So the purpose of this chapter is to make sure you learn all the techniques needed to align people around your company's core values.

PRACTICE #1: ALIGN THE CORE VALUES

....

The first quantum shift for leaders to make in their thinking is to recognize the importance of aligning everyone around the *company's* core values. These are the behaviors and activities essential to the organization's success. This is a significant departure from the traditional way of thinking about core values when people got together to talk about what behaviors were important to them. It is the leader's job to discover these fundamental core values and make them apparent to all. By doing so, you begin to instill deep feelings of trust, ownership, and mutual accountability.

As Larry Johnston, the CEO of Albertson's supermarket chain puts it: "There are two dimensions to leadership. Performance and values. You can't have one without the other."[3]

Before we go any further, let's be sure everyone understands what I mean by core values. For example, if I say my house has a lot of "value," it means my house is worth a lot of money. But that's not the same as a core value. If I say: "I value time with my friends," it means I enjoy spending time with them. But that's not the same as a core value. When I say, "I value my family," I am stating what is of utmost importance to me. That begins to capture the meaning of "core values."

BENEFITS OF CORE VALUES

	OPERATING WITH CORE VALUES	OPERATING WITHOUT CORE VALUES
EXTERNALLY	• People perceive the company as being motivated to do good. • Customers are drawn to the company's services and/or products. • The company is known for its integrity and innovation.	• People view the company as being self-serving. • Customers perceive little difference between the company and its competitors. • The company is known for being cautious, reactive.
INTERNALLY	• People operate out of trust. People raise uncomfortable issues and discuss them openly. • Decisions are decentralized. People feel empowered. • Innovation is encouraged. • Employees embrace change and adapt quickly. • Talented people are drawn to join the organization.	• Trust is low. People operate out of fear. People are reluctant to raise conflicts or sensitive issues. • Decisions are centralized. There's a culture of command and control. • Innovation is stifled. • Employees lack energy and motivation to change. • Talented people leave. Mediocrity prevails.

To make things more complex, there are different *systems* of values orbiting around us like electrons around a proton. First, we have our *personal values.* These are what we value most as an individual: survival comes first, followed by family, personal dignity, and freedom.[4] Beyond these lie other personal values. Some people value amassing a vast fortune. Others value public service. It's safe to assume that Donald Trump holds a different set of personal values than the pope.

Another layer of values is our *work values.* These are the things we consider important in our working lives. Some people value creativity. Others value teamwork. Some people value hard physical labor. Some value intellectual activity.

Orbiting around our personal and work values are *cultural values*. Cultural values vary greatly. Freedom of individual expression is highly valued in the United States. People in Denmark value egalitarianism. Deference to authority is valued in Saudi Arabia. A culture's values influence and permeate the people who live within it.[5]

Finally, there are the *company's core values*. When I talk about an organization's "core values," I'm referring to the things that are essential to its success, such as product reliability, customer satisfaction, and ethical integrity. These are the values that the organization, if it had a mind of its own, would say are essential to its long-term success.

THE LEADER AS STEWARD

Let's pause there for a moment. I said that the company's core values are what the company would say are the behaviors essential to its success. But the organization clearly has no voice. Or does it? What is the role of a leader if not to articulate what is most important to the organization itself? Effective leaders are stewards, doing whatever is necessary to develop and sustain the organization for a period of time and then turn it over to the next group of leaders in as good if not better shape than when they received it.

This notion of stewardship is critical. When the leaders in an organization view themselves as stewards, it enables them to take a longer view—and to put in place systems that will help the company grow, sustain, and endure. Google's core values reflect this kind of stewardship: (1) creativity and challenge; (2) unbiased, accurate, and free access to information; (3) independence and focused objectivity; (4) long-term financial sustainability; and (5) investment in talented employees. They define very clearly what activities and behaviors are essential for Google's success.

DEVELOPING CORE VALUES

If core values capture what's essential to the long-term, sustainable success of the organization, it makes sense that they need to be defined first, before anything else can be put into place. Before you decide where your company is going, you need to put your finger on the pulse of the company's core values. So how do you figure out the core values? Where do you look? What steps should you take? How do you begin the process?

Developing core values begins with exploring questions like these: "What did the people who came before us say? What do our founding documents say? What would someone who was acting in the best interest of this organization do to ensure its success?" This is the essence of John Rawls's "neutral man" standard, which he articulated in his groundbreaking book *A Theory of Justice*.[6] Defining your company's core values means taking the time to engage in a deep exploration of what truly is essential to its success.

Here's a trick: I've discovered that people need to explore certain broad *categories* of core values to make sure that they identify all the core values relevant to their organization. The following diagram shows these different categories.

Why these seven? Customer satisfaction and reliability are obvious, since they cut to the heart of attracting and retaining customers, regardless of your product or service. Ethical integrity is essential as well. Given the transparency revolution, companies simply risk too much by not behaving ethically. Attracting and retaining talented people is also essential. Safety is critical to success in many companies. And environmental protection, while at one time not viewed as an essential activity, is now seen by many companies to be a core value, both because it's the right thing to do and because damaging the environment can be ruinous to a company's reputation. And finally, financial sustainability is essential. Without financial resources, the enterprise cannot function.

In short, these broad categories of core values are a good starting point for exploring what is essential to the success of your organization. By exploring all of them, you can be sure that you've left no stone unturned. Knowing the broad categories is just the starting point, however. You must develop the details surrounding each core value, including the management and employee behaviors that support each core value (what I refer to as the "we statements"). You also have to peg the core values to a scorecard, so you can measure whether they're being achieved.

Here's a five-step process to help your organization define its core values.

STEP ONE: FORM THE CORE VALUES PLANNING TEAM

Defining the core values planning team is an all-important step, because the rest of the company will look to see whether this team owns the core values, consistently communicates them, and champions them when conflicts arise, as they inevitably will. In most cases, this team should consist of the senior-most leaders of the organization. After all, they're the current stewards of the enterprise. The CEO or top leader definitely needs to be a part of the planning team. This is not a job to delegate. His or her strong participation is crucial, given that the outcome will be the essential values and performance measures[7] for the company. If he or she chooses not to actively take part, it's a sure sign that the exercise is not serious.

STEP TWO: REFLECT ON THE CORE VALUES

The basic question is this: What activities are essential for our organization's success? In an earlier part of this chapter, I listed the seven categories of core values that one should explore. Use those seven categories to begin writing down your company's core values and detail some of the activities and behaviors that are essential to support it (the "we statements"). For example, for the core value of financial sustainability, supporting behaviors might be "maintaining competitive prices" or "assuring access to credit." The team should meet several times and generate a list of core values and supporting behaviors as shown in the example on the following page.

STEP THREE: IDENTIFY POTENTIAL CONFLICTS

Before you too quickly decide on a set of core values, you should talk about areas where conflict could occur between the core values. Not all core values will be in harmony with each other—some will be in discord. A core value of financial profitability will be discordant with a core value of customer satisfaction. Talk about cases where these conflicts have occurred—or might occur—between the values. For example, a planning team member might say: "We currently don't measure customer satisfaction in any rigorous, systematic way. To do so will be expensive. We assume it will pay off in increased customers and higher sales per customer. Those assumptions are untested. And it will put pressure on our core value of financial profitability."

Another planning team member might say: "It is not clear to me that doing no harm to the environment is a core value. It is not entirely within our span of control. There are things we may need to do that would conflict with this value. I want to see us motivated to do the right thing in making our decisions—but not at the expense of doing the smart thing for our company."

SUPPORTING BEHAVIORS FOR CORE VALUES

CORE VALUES	ORGANIZATIONAL BEHAVIORS
Financial Sustainability	• Profitability • Competitive prices • Credit rating • Return on capital • Return on investment
Customer Satisfaction	• Customer satisfaction • Customer "reference-ability" • Customer retention
Ethical Integrity	• Honesty • Responsibility • Fairness • Community service • Respect
Employee Satisfaction	• Workplace satisfaction • Attract and retain qualified employees • Diversity/inclusion
Reliability	• Reliable supply • Reliable quality
Safety	• Customer safety • Employee safety
Environmental Protection	• Protection of environment • Healthfulness of one's products and services • Promotion of cleaner environment

These are exactly the discussions you should be having at this point. Start to talk about how you might measure your success in achieving each core value (I'll talk more about that in a moment). Discuss how the team might need to communicate to resolve those conflicts. How should you make decisions when two or more core values are in tension? There's no right answer to the question. The right response is that you've thought it through and trust that you can communicate effectively with each other to strike the right balance.

STEP FOUR: LINK BEHAVIORS TO THE CORE VALUES

As you start to pin down your core values, it's important to list the management and employee behaviors that support them in the form of "we statements." In the example below, you can see how one company translated its core value of customer satisfaction into we statements.

LINKING BEHAVIORS TO CORE VALUES

CORE VALUE: CUSTOMER SATISFACTION
We communicate with our clients regularly and assure "no surprises."
When serving multiple clients, we communicate regularly with all of them.
We accomplish projects on deadline.
We accomplish projects within budget.
We are flexible and adapt to changes in our clients' needs and desires.
We communicate internally when a client's needs are not being met (e.g., deadlines, project completion, and budget).
We provide adequate time to get projects done.
We provide the resources to sustain and advance the firm.
We respond to all client calls and emails within twenty-four hours.
We regularly brainstorm innovative ways to serve our clients.
We keep each other informed about our clients' activities and about new clients.

Inevitably, someone will ask: "How many we statements do we need?" The answer is: "As many as there are behaviors that support the core value." Typically, there will be ten to fifteen we statements for each core value.

One note: You'll find yourself tempted to use the word "quality" in your we statements, as in: "We maintain quality customer service." There's a problem with this. Every single core value is about quality. My suggestion is to find words other than quality. And don't, by any means, create a separate category for quality. Down that road lies vast confusion!

STEP FIVE: DEFINE HOW TO MEASURE THE CORE VALUES

As you hone your core values, it's very helpful to discuss and define how you'll measure them. This is a critical step. By articulating how you'll measure your core values, you help make sure people understand what they mean. Ultimately, as the adage goes, what you measure is what you do. So metrics are key to aligning people around the core values.

What are some examples? Customer satisfaction can be measured by asking customers to rate your products or services. Competitive pricing can be measured via an index of competitors' prices. Reliability can be measured by the percentage of defects. Integrity can be measured by asking people what they think (your employees, your customers, your shareholders). Each value should be tied to a metric (what you'll measure) and a target (the desired level). The process of determining how to measure each value will help you clear away any lingering cobwebs about what the value means. For example, if innovation is a core value, then figuring out how to measure it will help clarify what it means. Is it generating new products and services? Is it being perceived as innovative by your customers? Is it continuous improvement in quality? There are many different ways to measure it.

THE BALANCED SCORECARD

Remember our definition: core values reflect what's essential to the success of the company. So in the process of linking specific performance metrics and targets to your core values, you are, in effect, creating a balanced performance scorecard for the organization. It's a scorecard that balances the competing values of cost effectiveness and customer satisfaction, of reliability and innovation.

CORE VALUES SCORECARD

CORE VALUES	METRICS	TARGETS
Financial Sustainability	• Keep prices competitive • Maintain access to credit • Preserve profit margin • Generate return on equity	• Retail prices average 5% below competitors' • Sales growth of 5% per year • Sales per customer up 2% each year • Minimum 7% profit margin • AAA rating from Moody's • ROE 11%
Reliability	• Sell defect-free products	• Fewer than 12 products returned for quality reasons per thousand sold
Customer Satisfaction	• Delight customers	• Composite customer satisfaction ratings over 95% • No single measure below 85%
Employee Satisfaction	• Attract and retain a productive workforce	• Score 85% or better in annual employee satisfaction survey
Ethical Integrity	• Be honest in all of our dealings with one another and with customers • Comply with conflict-of-interest code	• Zero tolerance for instances of dishonesty or noncompliance • Internal assessment over 95%
Environmental Protection	• Do no direct harm to the environment	• Zero tolerance for violation of applicable laws • Recycling equals 50% of total waste stream
Safety	• Protect the safety of our employees and customers	• Fewer than 1 safety incident per month for employees • Fewer than 1 safety incident per quarter per store for customers

AN EXAMPLE OF CORE VALUES

Here is an example of core values, taken from one of the most successful companies in the world. First, review the list of core values. Then I'll reveal the company.

CORE VALUES	SUPPORTING BEHAVIORS
People	• We attract and recruit the finest people in the world.
	• We build our organization from within, promoting and rewarding people without regard to any difference unrelated to performance.
	• We act on the conviction that the men and women of P&G will always be our most important asset.
Leadership	• We are all leaders in our area of responsibility, with a deep commitment to deliver leadership results.
	• We have a clear vision of where we are going.
	• We focus our resources to achieve leadership objectives and strategies.
	• We develop the capability to deliver our strategies and eliminate organizational barriers.
Ownership	• We accept personal accountability to meet the business needs, improve our systems, and help others improve their effectiveness.
	• We all act like owners, treating the company's assets as our own and behaving with the company's long-term success in mind.
Integrity	• We always try to do the right thing.
	• We are honest and straightforward with each other.
	• We operate within the letter and spirit of the law.
	• We uphold the values and principles of P&G in every action and decision.
	• We are data-based and intellectually honest in advocating proposals, including recognizing risks.

(continued)

CORE VALUES	SUPPORTING BEHAVIORS
Trust	• We are determined to be the best at doing what matters most. • We have a healthy dissatisfaction with the status quo. • We have a compelling desire to improve and to win in the marketplace.
Passion for Winning	• We respect our P&G colleagues, customers, and consumers and treat them as we want to be treated. • We have confidence in each other's capabilities and intentions. • We believe that people work best when there is a foundation of trust.

By now, you may have guessed what P&G stands for. Procter & Gamble is one of the world's leading makers of consumer products. With billions in sales, P&G has a reputation for excellence in marketing.[8] It is a company whose leaders have assured its enduring success by continually reaffirming and communicating its core values.

Having a balanced scorecard will also help you address your critics. For example, some people might voice concerns about financial performance. Yes, you might respond, we could have higher levels of profits in the short term by cutting employees, but our service and reliability measures would decline—and ultimately our customers would start to leave and revenues would erode. Does operating that way somehow increase profitability?

My bias, based on my experiences, is that the financial performance results are universally positive when a company aligns its people around core values. At a grocery chain, for instance, profits rose 24 percent the year after our firm facilitated the introduction of a core values–based management system. At a $200 million software company where we did this, profits rose 37 percent.

Once you've defined your scorecard, waste no time in starting to communicate it. The CEO of one of our clients, a large energy company, insists that the scorecard be communicated to shareholders, customers, and employees every month. This is the most important thing that leaders can do to align everyone in the organization around the core values. Public communication about the scorecard builds trust that leaders are holding themselves—and everyone else—accountable. Remember, it is okay for the company to fail to hit its performance targets. People can accept that. What they cannot accept is a lack of transparency—or being held to performance standards by bosses who themselves are not held accountable. Though this point is intuitively obvious, how many leaders have failed to grasp this most fundamental idea? I can think of a few!

COMMUNICATE THE CORE VALUES

Once the core values are defined, it's important to engage managers and employees in understanding them. This will build buy-in. It will also give you an opportunity to communicate what you're doing and why. People need to hear that you are intent on building a values-based, performance-driven organization.

This education process should be conceived as a campaign designed to accomplish three things: (1) engaging people, (2) stimulating additional discussion and brainstorming, and (3) communicating how the core values will be used and measured.

This takes time and energy. But it's well worth it. People should be encouraged to fully discuss and understand the values. Not everyone will get it at first—but that's okay. Strive for 90 percent. The rest will eventually get it—or get weeded out.

The CEO or top leader needs to be fully involved in the education process. His or her leadership in the process is symbolically crucial and is the catalyst needed to build ownership of the values at each level. For example, a financial services company in Los Angeles came up with three core values: Purpose, People, and Passion. Each of these was tied to "we statements." The CEO then spent several months communicating these core values, making sure they were integrated into everything from the company's recruiting to its employee satisfaction survey.

As you're educating people about the core values, make it a big deal. We've seen leaders translate them into banners, post them in every meeting room, incorporate them into stationery. In one case, the CEO had a new sign erected in front of the headquarters with the core values emblazoned on it. The day the sign was unveiled, he stood at the entrance, shook every employee's hand, gave them a matching lapel pin, and said: "These are our values: when you enter here, know that these are the things that guide us in everything we do."

But that's not enough.

THE FOUR CONVERSATIONS

Through trial and error, I've discovered that four conversations are necessary before everyone truly feels aligned with—and committed to—their organization's core values.

The first conversation is how each person interprets the core values. You begin by handing people a copy of the core values and then asking a simple question: "Would you agree that these are the things most essential to our organization's success?"

This conversation enables people to discover their common ground—and areas of disagreement. The disagreement is healthy and critical, for it furnishes an opportunity for important dialogue and a chance for people to discover a deeper connection to the value than first appeared. The danger is not that people won't unite around the core values; it's that they will unite too quickly, thus avoiding the tough conversations that build understanding and trust.

The second conversation explores the difference between organizational core values and personal core values. This discussion is best handled by asking people to say: "What's most important to you, personally? How does it tie to the organization's core values?" This conversation enables people to articulate their own values (often for the first time). It gives people a chance to know one another, to appreciate their differences, and to reflect on the fact that their differences are born of deeply held beliefs. For example, an employee of a large retail chain said his greatest passion was painting natural landscapes. He then pointed out that his love of painting shared a surprising connection with excellent customer service. "You have to find hidden delight in each and every encounter," he said.

CORE VALUES EXAMPLE: STARBUCKS

....

Starbucks is a good example of an organization that is clear about its core values. It has six:

1. Provide a great work environment and treat each other with respect and dignity;
2. Embrace diversity as an essential component in the way we do business;
3. Apply the highest standards of excellence to the purchasing, roasting, and fresh delivery of our coffee;
4. Develop enthusiastically satisfied customers all the time;
5. Contribute positively to our communities and our environment;
6. Recognize that profitability is essential to our future success.

At Starbucks, performance is measured on the basis of these core values. The information is translated into a scorecard and readily shared with managers, who in turn brainstorm ways to continually improve. All decisions are driven by these core values. The result? Starbucks has enjoyed extraordinary growth because it could maintain the quality of both its customer service and its products while opening more than 7,200 stores—a remarkable feat of decentralization.

The third conversation applies the organization's values to real cases. It's constructive to look back at times when the organization was not true to its values. Without casting blame, people can ask what happened. Looking forward, they can anticipate scenarios in which the values might again be challenged.

The conversation can begin by asking: "Looking at how we've defined the organization's core values, think of a time when we did not uphold these. What happened? How did we make decisions that led us to that point? What could we do differently in the future in our communication and decision making to forestall it from happening again?"

The final conversation is translating the core values into performance objectives for each job classification. People need to understand that the "we statements" are not philosophical fluff—they will be appraised based on how closely their behaviors align with the behaviors tied to each core value. This is what creates a powerful linkage and an integrated performance management system.

"HOLLOW" VALUES

When you're defining an organization's core values, it's critical to avoid making them sound hollow. Here's one set of core values defined by a corporation that looks good on paper, but doesn't stand up to scrutiny:

- We work as a team.
- We act with integrity and honesty.
- We champion and celebrate diversity.
- We expect and support exceptional service.
- We celebrate our successes.
- We encourage creativity and innovation.
- We care about our community.

This list has three problems: First, there's no definition of what these things are or what they mean. Are they the behaviors essential for the company's success? Are they behaviors that are important to a team? Second, some core values appear to be missing, such as financial sustainability. Last, some things seem to belong to others. For example, "we celebrate successes" seems to belong with "we work as a team." It should come as no surprise that this particular set of values had little impact on this organization.

Here's another example of what I consider to be hollow values from Jamba Juice, a health-oriented seller of fruit-based shakes and other products:

Fun—Have fun. Smile and create a spirit of celebration for your customers.

Integrity—Do what you say. Demonstrate good character and encourage an atmosphere of mutual trust and respect.

Balance—Live a balanced life. Consider the needs of customers, team members, and shareholders alike.

Empowerment—Believe in yourself. Be responsive and innovative. Do whatever it takes to make your customer happy.

Respect—Be respectful. Help each other to grow. Contribute to a vibrant and diverse community.

The sentiment behind these values is heartfelt, but the values don't reflect all that is essential to Jamba Juice. Choosing company values based on the initial letters of the words makes the words themselves feel trite. You need to listen carefully for clues that your organization has failed to engage in a deep examination of the organization's core values. If you sense this, resolve to do something about it right away. Nothing is more harmful to a company's morale than the appearance that its leaders gave too little thought to what makes the company successful.

USE VALUES TO DECENTRALIZE DECISIONS

One of the greatest benefits of developing a framework of core values is that decision making can be decentralized. When people understand the company's core values, there is no need for top-down command and control. Instead, you can implement "values-based decision making." The result can be higher levels of innovation, performance, and creativity. In the early days of Southwest Airlines, Herb Kelleher and his management team wanted to reduce the turnaround time for aircraft on the ground. They set a goal of fifteen minutes. They got it down to ten. Kelleher describes watching in awe as the maintenance supervisors and frontline employees came up with innovation after innovation to meet what was seen as an impossible standard. How did they do it? Southwest had already established a culture of decentralized decision making and performance. What was standard at Southwest was the exception elsewhere.

The tension between centralization and decentralization tends to disappear when values-based decision making is in place. One California state agency, for example, articulated its core values and tied them to performance measures. The result? Dozens of new entrepreneurial ideas sprang up, with far less need for centralized check-off or intervention.

On the other hand, when core values are missing, bureaucracy and centralization tend to take over. One software company insisted on a uniform hardware and software platform for every single employee, despite the differences in end users' needs. Customers complained about poor customer service; financial performance plummeted. A "black market" emerged to address the problem, creating further internal tensions. Lacking an explicit framework, the *de facto* values continued to reign, with the press for uniformity trumping employee innovation, trust, and satisfaction.

In short, the link between core values and decentralized decision making is one of the most powerful arguments for this first quantum shift. Successful leaders should strive to instill a culture of values-based decision making throughout their organizations. When they do, the results can be extraordinary.

As you align the core values, look around and see what remnants of older thinking you can get rid of. Ask yourself whether the following systems need to be retooled to make them consistent with your organization's core values:

- Reporting systems—the organizational structure and hierarchy
- Executive perks
- Hiring practices and systems
- Training systems
- Compensation systems
- Performance review systems
- Internal communication systems
- Information technology systems
- Rules on information access and disclosure

As you align people around the company's core values, you'll find that each of these systems needs tweaking. For example, your compensation guidelines will need to be modified to reward people who uphold the core values. Communication systems need to default to sharing, not hoarding, key information about company performance. Training workshops need to build competencies that align with the core values. Once you set these wheels in motion, it can take a year to get all your systems aligned. The fun is in seeing it materialize in the form of higher levels of trust.

• • •

CONCLUSION

Effective leaders who want to generate lasting, sustained success in their organizations spend a considerable amount of time and energy clarifying and communicating the strategic focus of the organization. They understand that it is the first step in building the levels of trust needed to get people to do their best. Good leaders devote considerable energy and time to a deep examination of the organization's core values. By doing so, they get to the heart of what is essential for the customers and shareholders— and thus essential for success. This is true whether you're a small company or a large one, a nonprofit, or a public entity. Communicating the core values creates powerful alignment across departments and divisions. This yields clarity of focus and enables people to make better decisions, consistently, across long spans of time.

Core values are not mysterious. Typical core values include things like ethical integrity, customer service, product excellence, and environmental stewardship. The hard work is in communicating them consistently, day after day, so that a culture of respect is built around them. Creating this kind of culture is crucial for building trust.

SHARPEN THE FOCUS

(ACV+STF+LTO+MDW+SWY) + (APC+SCF+SST+MTC+APQ) = LC

IBM's former CEO Louis Gerstner orchestrated a remarkable turn-around of IBM. How did he do it? By sharpening the focus. Gerstner's vision for IBM was to fulfill customers' needs instead of create the next new technology.

A simple idea, but a revolution at IBM.

In the early 1980s, before Gerstner arrived, Big Blue had been trying to establish its own operating system as a standard for mainframes. Taking its cue from the breakup of AT&T into "Baby Bells," plans were afoot to break up Big Blue into several "Baby Blues" in order to extract more shareholder value from the company.

When Gerstner arrived, he saw IBM's problem as a lack of focus on the one thing that matters: customers and the value you provide them. He saw the breakup of IBM as a big mistake. He thought it would destroy IBM's ability to provide integrated solutions to customers on a global scale.[1]

Gerstner became preoccupied with understanding IBM's customers and their changing needs. Over a six-month period, he logged more than a million miles of air travel as part of this quest. As a result of Gerstner's leadership, IBM focused on providing customers with solutions, regardless of whether those solutions were proprietary to IBM. Its vaunted operating systems division was closed down, and a new global services division erected in its place.

Effective leaders give their organizations this kind of sharp strategic vision. When Gerstner said, "We're going to shed any part of our company that doesn't put customers first," he was serious. When employees asked where they would fit in the new organizational chart, he told them, "You're asking the wrong question. You should be focused on customers, not yourself." And then he shut down the department responsible for making organizational charts!

As a result of Gerstner's zeal, IBM's revenues climbed steadily, reversing what had been a moribund course. From 1992 to 2001, Gerstner's strategy resulted in something on the order of $152 billion in value, if one looks at the rise in IBM's market capitalization over that period.

Sharpening the focus will fuel your organization's success, too. In my experience, organizations with a sharp focus will always outperform the rest. From Google to Starbucks, from Curves to Southwest Airlines, organizations that operate with a sense of focus deliver higher value to their customers and shareholders and create an environment in which employees feel high levels of trust and spark. By definition, when people are focused, they're less likely to get distracted by the petty stuff.

How do you do this? How do you enable your people to see exactly what they need to accomplish and how they fit into the big picture? That's what we're going to look at in this chapter. As I did in the last chapter, I'll take you through the process step by step. But let me first explain how this process works to help build trust.

Great leaders build trust by defining vision. People want to know that there's a plan and a direction. Vision has two components. The *external vision* defines the outcomes that the company wants to achieve. Southwest Airlines' vision is to make air travel cheaper and more convenient than auto travel. Curves' vision is to make it affordable and easy for women to be physically fit. HSBC Bank's vision is to be the world's local bank.

The second component is an *internal plan* of change. Vision needs to be linked to a clear understanding of what needs to happen to achieve it. Sometimes it means a small shift in focus and direction. Sometimes it means redeploying current assets in new ways. Occasionally it requires a full-scale revamping of the company's business model. Here are the four crucial steps to develop a fully understood and fully realized vision.

PRACTICE #2: SHARPEN THE FOCUS

It is not good enough to communicate a vague sense of direction—to talk, for example, about being the world leader in your industry. People want a more focused vision: What is the future your company wants to create? What will your company do to revolutionize how your customers live, work, or play? How specifically will you make the world a better place? Sharpening the focus is not easy. It requires difficult, sometimes painful choices. But a sharp strategic focus will build trust (and generate spark). Research has shown that the more focused the vision is, the more people will dedicate themselves to achieving it.

STEP 1: DEFINE THE VISION

Defining the vision and capturing it in writing is simple to say, but hard to do. Begin by asking the following: Who do we want to engage in this process of defining our vision? What's the brain trust I need? Do we need outside resources to help stimulate our thinking and keep us on track?

In many cases, this planning team consists of the CEO and his or her executive team. In others, it may involve members of your board of directors or outside stakeholders. You want people with thoughtful insights into your industry, people with different points of view who can listen and change minds. Above all, you want the key people in your company who will follow through and champion the vision and the resulting plan.

Once you've identified this planning team, here are some initial questions for it to consider:

1. What are our primary customer segments today—the people for whom we are trying to create the most value? What will they be in five years or ten years? (Pick a planning horizon.)

2. What is our current business model? How does it translate into profitability? How will it change in five years?

3. What trends are affecting our customers? How will they perceive the value of our products and services changing over the next five years?

4. What alternatives to our products and services do our customers have? How are those alternatives changing?

5. Are we focusing on the right customers? Are our competitors also focused on the same customers? What would happen if we shifted our customer focus?

6. What could we do more of (or less of) to create increased value for our customers?

7. What might be some essential innovations in our way of doing business that would create added value for our customers? How could we redefine our way of doing business?

8. Based on the above, what should be our vision? What outcomes are we trying to achieve? What are the rationales for that vision?

9. Based on the above, what is our internal plan—how do we envision our organization changing over the next five years to support our vision?

10. What are the major priorities for change and investment we need to make in order to realize that vision?

BENEFITS OF STRATEGIC FOCUS

STRATEGIC FOCUS IS WELL UNDERSTOOD	STRATEGIC FOCUS IS NOT UNDERSTOOD
People embrace change and adapt their jobs accordingly.	People lack energy or motivation to change.
People measure themselves by how well they and their teams perform.	People measure themselves by achieving tasks—or not at all.
People take initiative.	People are reactive.
People raise uncomfortable issues and discuss them openly.	People are reluctant to raise conflicts or sensitive issues.
Morale is high, and turnover is correspondingly low.	Morale tends to be low and turnover high.

At some point, you'll need to agree on the planning horizon (i.e., a time period for which you're trying to plan). For some organizations, vision spans a ten- to fifteen-year period. But in others a shorter horizon—three or five years—is more fitting. At Teradyne, a fast-moving maker of software that monitors web performance, the planning horizon was one year. Why? Because the software industry was moving so quickly its CEO didn't see any value in setting a vision beyond the next twelve months.

As you listen to people's visions, it's valuable to write them down on paper and try to isolate the key variables. One way we do this is by developing "strategy maps" and scenarios, showing how significant business variables translate into different visions. As people discuss their scenarios, you can begin to draw out their different visions and compare them.

One of my favorite examples of scenario planning is the city of Portland, Oregon. The city did an extraordinary thing when it was developing its twenty-five-year plan back in the 1970s. It asked citizens to think about values like open space, affordable housing, job creation, clean air, and urban density. Based on these results, city planners then constructed hypothetical scenarios for the future of Portland.

One scenario emphasized economic development and job creation, one scenario emphasized preserving open space, and one scenario emphasized affordable housing. Each of the visions reflected a different weighting of values. Portland's planning staff then surveyed citizens and asked them to rank the scenarios from most favorite to least favorite. Citizens responded in high numbers. They indicated that preserving open space was their highest priority, followed by job creation.

Portland's city planners then came up with a plan that imposed a tight restriction on growth outside a well-defined urban core. There was room for some development—but not much. Citizens had indicated they were willing to put up with the higher housing prices and higher urban densities that this plan would necessitate—in exchange for increased protection of open space.

Today, visitors to Portland can see the impact of this long-range vision—and the success it generated. A lovely green ring of open space surrounds Portland. Its economy has boomed. Its housing values have skyrocketed—and new housing units are built in high densities. Unlike most cities, where trade-offs this complex are simply not addressed or brought to a vote, Portland illustrates the value of tackling questions of vision head on.

A VISION EXERCISE

....

Here's an exercise to get your different visions on the table.

Envision yourself five years from now (or whatever your planning horizon). Imagine you are reading a newspaper article about your company. The article talks about the remarkable success your organization has achieved. Imagine the headline and the story that accompanies the headline.

Write down the headline and the story in your own words. In the story, what were the most important decisions that propelled the company to this success? Who made them? What specific things did the company do? Talk about what conflicts it had to resolve along the way.

When people are ready, ask them to share their headlines and stories. Once they've done so, ask people to comment on the stories and talk about what they like and dislike. Ask them to focus on what excites them about the various visions.

After this exercise, ask people which visions are most compelling. At this point, one or two visions will emerge. Then ask people to look at the visions in two ways. First, emotionally: "Does this excite you?" Second, analytically: "What are the rationales for doing this? What's the value to our customers? What's the benefit to them? The benefit to the company?"

Keep asking those questions and eliciting responses until people converge around a common vision.

STEP 2: SHARPEN THE VISION

Nothing can be a priority if everything is. To sharpen the focus, you need to make clear what the organization will *not* do and what is *not* a priority. A nationwide chain of auto parts stores planned to open an average of one new store a month for two years. The CEO told his managers: "We are not considering any mergers or acquisitions. We need to devote all our energy to supporting the new stores."

Some leaders prefer not to sharpen the focus, assuming it gives them increased flexibility to respond to opportunities. But when vision is fuzzy, trust goes in the tank. Major conflicts go unaddressed. Politics can supersede performance. Bureaucracy can trump innovation. People's cheater meters are constantly going off as they sense a lack of real leadership.

When the focus is fuzzy, bad things can happen. Here's one example.

For nearly one hundred years, Sears, Roebuck was the greatest catalog retailer in the world. It exemplified innovation and customer service. As a result, its financial house was in order. Then in the early 1980s, Sears started to diversify into higher-margin, unrelated financial services in order to boost its stock price. Its vision became muddied. Was it to be the innovator in low-price retailing? Was it to be the premier catalog marketer—which would have positioned it perfectly for e-commerce? No, its vision was to make more money.

Because its vision was primarily financial, Sears lost sight of its catalog and retail business. Wal-Mart and others came along and created retail alternatives in rural areas. Through innovations of their own, they found ways to improve margins and create greater profits. Once that occurred, Sears's vaunted combination of service, quality, and pricing started to crumble. It became just another retailer—and in the process lost billions of dollars in shareholder value.

Another example of fuzzy vision is America Online (AOL). In the early 1990s, AOL was battling early online entrants like Prodigy and CompuServe for dominant share of the digital information business. The merger with Time Warner was seven years away. Over the next six years, AOL grew explosively. Steve Case, the cofounder of AOL, built partnerships with information providers, grew subscribers, and extolled the importance of "content communities." At the pinnacle of the first dot-com boom in 2000, AOL bought Time Warner. Steve Case became a billionaire.

But then came the fall. Coincident with the merger with Time Warner, AOL lost its focus on being the best online information provider. It instead tried to build shareholder value through marketing partnerships. It sold advertising packages that annoyed subscribers and provided little or no value to the consumer or to the buyer of the ad.

When the hoped-for synergies with Time Warner's traditional content failed to materialize, AOL's focus became very fuzzy indeed. Talented people came and went. The Internet bubble burst. AOL came under a cloud for phony revenue reporting. The stock price declined dramatically. Steve Case was forced out, the victim of fuzzy vision.

To be successful, a vision must meet five "tests":

1. It must capture an understanding of what the company can be great at.

2. It must make clear how the organization will deliver values to its customers in ways that are compelling and different from the competition.

3. It must be measurable—people need to know whether the company is on course to achieve the vision.

4. It must translate into a clear and compelling message, both in writing and when spoken. If it's not easy to communicate, if you can't create a clear mental picture of it, then you need to work some more.

5. It must also be achievable—you must be able to translate it into a plan of action.

Successful visions meet this five-way test. Google's founders, Larry Page and Sergey Brin, published an "owner's manual" in conjunction with the company's initial public offering in 2004. They began by saying: "Google is not a conventional company. We do not intend to become one." They concluded with this vision: "We believe strongly that in the long term, we will be better served—as shareholders and in all other ways—by a company that does good things for the world even if we forgo some short-term gains."[2]

STEP 3: COMMUNICATE THE VISION

Once you've defined the vision, you need to communicate it across the organization and align every business unit. A strong vision is inevitably based on certain assumptions about the future. The leader's job is to explain those assumptions and then lay out the vision and the benefits associated with it, and contrast them to the consequences of inaction.

In communicating vision, you have to satisfy five critical concerns:

1. The leaders of the company are seriously committed and engaged in achieving the vision
2. No one is exempt from change; everyone is part of the effort
3. The benefits are large
4. The risk of failure is shared
5. There is a plan

Avoid the trap of having too many goals at once. This saps the focus and dulls people's energies. One CEO had fourteen goals for her company. When asked why, she remarked: "It's important to me that everyone have a goal that reflects what they do." Talk about fuzzy focus! Sharpening the focus means establishing priorities not recognizing everyone's pet project.

STEP 4: DEVELOP A SCORECARD

A strong vision is tied to a specific plan with clear goals, objectives, and timetables. For example, if the vision is to enter a new market, then the plan might be to establish a beachhead office there, or to introduce a product that will attract sales in that market. If your vision is to become more vertically integrated, then one goal might be to make acquisitions to complete your vertical portfolio. What's important is using the vision as a litmus test to plan the use of the organization's resources. When every manager is using the vision to set his or her business goals and budgets, then you'll know you've successfully sharpened the focus.

To make the vision real, people need quantifiable measures and targets to aim for. They need a scorecard. Real trust can only grow when people know how the organization's performance will be judged. In my experience, people align themselves around whatever is being measured like particles of iron around a magnet. That's why the scorecard is such a critical part of sharpening the focus.

A scorecard needs to capture three different dimensions:

- What will be measured (the metric)
- What you'll aim for (the target)
- The current performance (the baseline)

When measuring success, distinguish between inputs, activities, outputs, and outcomes. Outcomes measure the actual value you're creating, like satisfied customers or financial profitability, and they are the key to high performance. This is shown here in the "stairway to performance."

STAIRWAY TO PERFORMANCE

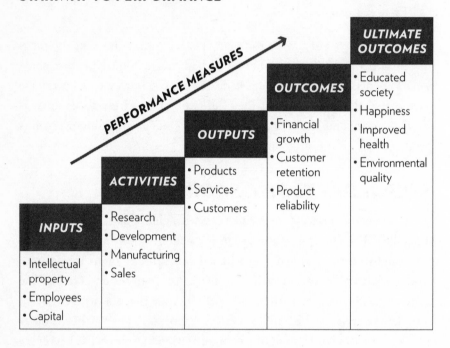

Too often I find organizations where leaders are deep in the weeds, tracking the number of sales calls per salesperson or the quantity of units produced, not the results in terms of satisfied customers, retention of key clients, or profitability. Not only does this produce skewed performance measures but it also breeds turf battles. So when you're putting together your scorecard, make sure you're focusing on the right stuff.

The following table shows how a leader might translate his vision into a scorecard.

Done well, your performance scorecard will accelerate the pace of change and focus everyone's attention on how to improve the organization's performance. We'll talk about this more in Chapter 5.

BUILDING A PERFORMANCE SCORECARD

GOAL	PERFORMANCE METRIC	12-MONTH PERFORMANCE TARGET
Enter new markets	Number of customers in new markets	Customers from new markets equal 5 percent of total customers
	Profits from new markets	Gross profit margins from new market sales are 10 percent higher than our traditional business

THE BOARD OF DIRECTORS

So far, we've assumed the CEO and executive team are the ones sharpening the focus. But boards of directors have the ultimate decision-making authority in many companies and organizations. So if the problem is a lack of focus, how do you engage the board in sharpening it?

In private and public corporations, the CEO typically sits on the board and has a large influence on its decisions. So the process is similar to what I described earlier. But in public agencies, the chief executive does not typically sit on the board. Instead, an independently appointed or elected governing body holds responsibility for setting the vision. In those cases, the approach we prefer is for the board to communicate its vision through a linked set of written strategic policies. We strongly recommend that all public boards of directors develop policies that define in writing exactly what the board does and what results it wants the organization to achieve. These governance policies should be organized in a clear, coherent framework.

We've worked with many boards, drafting governance frameworks and policies. Once these policies are in place, the board can begin performing at a much higher level. It will hold itself more accountable—and staff more accountable. It will stop meddling in staff's decisions, giving staff the confidence they need to implement the strategic goals. With a scorecard and regular monitoring plan in place, the board can begin monitoring the performance of the organization in a systematic way. In a relatively short period of time, the organization can shift from underperforming to high performing.

NICHE VISION

There's a cartoon in my office that illustrates one of the basic tenets of strategic focus. The cartoon shows a large fishing net. On one side of the net swims a huge fish. On the other side swim a school of small fish. The caption reads: "Attention all fish: How to escape being trapped by a net: 'Either get so big you can bust the net, or stay small so you can swim right through.'" The lesson? It's dangerous to be a medium-sized fish.

Niche and Grow Rich[3] is a book that illustrates how e-commerce has created an explosion in small, niche businesses. The authors describe a man who made a successful business selling unicycles online. They talk about the huge number of online jewelry vendors—"digital gypsies." Whether you have an interest in garden railroads or traveling by barge through France, there's a niche company (or several of them) to serve you.

A sharply focused niche company enjoys several strategic advantages:

1. It can start small and stay small while maintaining an attractive profit margin.

2. Because of its size, it can adapt quickly to changes in the market and offer cutting-edge services and products that a larger competitor cannot.

3. It can be an attractive "roll-up" opportunity for an investor (who wants to combine several niche players), thus providing a handsome financial return for the founder-owners.

But there are downsides to niche companies too. Personality conflicts can wreak havoc on small companies. The lack of defined business processes can make it expensive to orient new people. The lack of objective marketing data may leave them vulnerable to shifts in consumer taste. I'm also struck by the fact that if all you're doing is selling unicycles, you'd better *love* unicycling.

• • •

CONCLUSION

There are four key dimensions to developing high-performing organizations: strategic focus, leadership development, process improvement, and performance measurement. In this chapter, we've focused on sharpening the strategic focus and measuring performance. As we move into the next chapters, we'll look at how to get the right people in place and further mold a leadership culture. But remember, it all begins with these first two steps: aligning people around the core values and sharpening the focus. Without those steps, you won't know what leadership capabilities you need or how to effectively measure performance.

This chapter began with the story of how Louis Gerstner sharpened the focus for IBM by visiting with customers for six months. He was on the road every week, listening to what customers had to say. His zeal translated into specific goals in the four main divisions of IBM. Each goal was linked to measurable performance objectives. When you consider that IBM had 140,000 employees at the time, finding focus took a lot of hard work. But it paid off for him, just as it can pay off for you.

LEAD THROUGH OTHERS

(ACV+STF+LTO+MDW+SWY) + (APC+SCF+SST+MTC+APQ) = LC

In the early 2000s, energy deregulation took place in California, triggering shock waves across the state. So how did the different utilities respond?

At the Sacramento Municipal Utility District, the board of directors and management team saw the changes coming and focused on purchasing long-term energy contracts. As a result, SMUD maintained stable rates. SMUD also built a suite of cleaner, cheaper generation facilities. In contrast, Pacific Gas & Electric reacted more complacently. Pressured by the legislature, PG&E sold off its generation facilities. To preserve its profits, PG&E entered into short-term energy contracts. These decisions sent PG&E scrambling when energy prices spiked. The result? PG&E began hemorrhaging money and in 2001 went bankrupt. Meanwhile, SMUD kept its electricity rates 25 percent lower than PG&E, and outperformed PG&E in every other meaningful category.

One could argue that these different outcomes were a result of external pressures. But SMUD had a dynamic management team. People were able to ask tough questions of one another. SMUD's leaders were focused on the long-term needs of their customers. PG&E's management team, on the other hand, didn't take a long-term perspective. It was preoccupied with preserving what it had. Unfortunately, the world had changed—and the failure to recognize that wound up costing PG&E ratepayers billions of dollars.

PRACTICE #3: LEAD THROUGH OTHERS

....

To understand the difference between a great company and a mediocre one, take a look at its people. Do they know their roles? Are they cast in the right roles? Are they clear on the results the company is trying to achieve? Do they know their decision-making authority? Do they work collaboratively and build trust with one another?

High-performing organizations don't occur by accident. The story of SMUD illustrates the value of hiring talented people, arming them with clear goals, and giving them the leeway to do their jobs. Because SMUD invested in a deep bench of talented managers and employees, it minimized bureaucracy and built a culture of engagement, trust, and innovation. Over the long run, this has saved SMUD millions of dollars.

This chapter will focus on the value of leading through others. You'll learn how to hire effective people, put them in the right roles, and empower them to lead—all of which helps build a system of trust.

THREE LEADERSHIP STYLES

Over the years I've identified three overall styles of leadership. Only one of these styles genuinely reflects the approach of leading through others.

The first style is the "Genius with a Thousand Helpers." This kind of "me" leader needs to make every decision—and grows defensive when his or her authority is challenged. The result is a military-like organizational structure. The Genius with a Thousand Helpers can be successful in attracting talented people. But since there's very little delegation of responsibility, the talented people eventually leave.

The Genius with a Thousand Helpers encourages the notion that the leader, the "genius," is the smartest kid in the room. In so doing, they exploit a well-known phenomenon called the "fundamental attribution error," which causes people to overemphasize the importance of the leader in making decisions. When the leader is not there to make a decision, everything grinds to a halt. People like Donald Trump have built careers off the fundamental attribution error.

The "Aloof Executive" is the exact opposite of the Genius with a Thousand Helpers. The Aloof Executive doesn't exert enough control. People head off in their own directions and become confused about their roles and responsibilities. With people doing their own thing, poor decisions get made. Eventually the Aloof Executive is surprised to find that things have gone horribly wrong. Instead of trying to change his own behaviors, he simply gets rid of the offenders, hires new people, and starts the pattern all over again.

The final style is called the "Balanced Leader." The orientation of the Balanced Leader is like the conductor of a jazz ensemble. Balanced Leaders understand they set the tempo and choreograph the underlying key changes, and then let the musicians improvise. Balanced Leaders view other people as centers of intelligence, whose ideas and contributions are essential if the organization is to thrive. Balanced Leaders create a level of delegation and support for those around them that enables people to carry out important initiatives. This results in a team-based environment in which everyone's leadership skills can shine.

When the fur is flying, the Balanced Leader asserts more control. But only temporarily. The Balanced Leader is quick to lead through others again once the "all clear" is signaled. Make no mistake, this kind of balanced approach takes time and practice—when to exert control, when to lay back. As Dizzy Gillespie put it, "It's taken me all my life to learn what notes not to play."[1]

DELEGATING EFFECTIVELY

To lead through others means you have to delegate. But most people don't know how. In fact, they don't know what they don't know about delegations. They talk in vague generalities and ask people to get things done. But they do so without clearly describing the purview of decision-making authority. They lack the vocabulary and systems of communication to be clear. As a result, I see people in companies floundering all the time. (This is what makes our job as organizational coaches so much fun!)

The next chapter will look in depth at decision making—and at the importance of distinguishing different levels of delegation. But here's a quick preview of an important tool.

The first level of delegation ("A") means that I've delegated to you the responsibility to take the initiative to recommend how to get something done. Your job is to gather the right people together, work up the options, figure out the best option, and bring to me a recommendation for my review and approval. Once I approve it, you're charged with implementing it.

The second level of delegation ("B") has the same responsibilities as in "A"—plus the added authority to make the decision on the recommendation and put it into effect. All I ask is that you notify me after the fact so that I know what's going on.

The third level of delegation ("C") has the same responsibilities as "B"—but I don't require you to notify me of your decision.

The best leaders, those who want to lead through others, use this type of framework to continually clarify how decisions are being made. The level of delegated authority will depend on many factors—but ultimately it will boil down to the importance of the decision and the level of trust you place in the person's decision-making abilities.

Our team of consultants has worked with dozens of clients to improve the clarity of delegations. By defining delegations clearly, communication, accountability, and performance will all improve. One example is a large state agency that evolved from a highly centralized to a distributed system of decision making, resulting in far more efficiency in delivering programs. Once managers clearly understood the levels of delegation and were empowered to lead, turnaround time on projects improved dramatically and financial performance skyrocketed. And the hemorrhaging of talent stopped almost overnight, creating a much deeper leadership "bench."

HIGH-PERFORMING TEAMS

One of the distinctions between good leaders and so-so leaders is the way in which they build effective teams. Southwest's "ten-minute turn" illustrates what happens when you build effective teams and enable them to push the boundaries. Initially, it was considered impossible to turn a jet around for another flight in under thirty minutes. Today, each Southwest jet is fueled and serviced, has its tires changed, and is ready to go in ten minutes. Initially, Southwest had to do it because it had only three jets for four routes. Today it does it because it can—and because it provides tremendous competitive advantage.

Patrick Lencioni has defined an effective way of thinking about the habits of highly effective teams.[2] We use his model in our work. Working with a team, we start at the bottom of the chart and keep clarifying until all five habits are in place.

FIVE HABITS OF HIGHLY EFFECTIVE TEAMS

....

1. **Attention to results:** Team members regularly monitor their progress toward achieving the results. They don't gloss over their performance, but talk about it.
2. **Accountability:** Team members hold each other accountable for their performance. When someone underperforms, the team tells them immediately and in direct, honest terms.
3. **Commitment:** Everyone adopts a common goal or set of goals and commits to achieving them. Goals are defined simply enough to be easily grasped, specific enough to be actionable.
4. **Creative conflict:** People ask tough questions of one another and challenge each other's assumptions. They probe an argument until they are satisfied.
5. **Trust:** Team members open up to each other. They admit their mistakes, weaknesses, and concerns without fear of reprisal.

When any of the five habits are missing, then trust is broken. There's no shame in admitting it. Effective leaders don't let their teams stay broken for long. They take the time to communicate and regenerate the sense of team trust. They get the critical issues on the table. They work through the checklist of five habits. They invest time and energy into making their teams effective again.

Before we leave this topic, let me add a final note that may sound like heresy: The word "team" is overused. A team, as I define it, is a set of people who convene to achieve a goal or set of goals. A team has the authority necessary to carry out its task and has clear measurements of progress. The members of a team must work together to achieve the goals. Compare that to a "group," which may not always comprise a team. A group is made up of people who share a common purpose but different objectives. For example, a group of managers may meet to share information and best practices, but may not be dependent on one another to achieve their goals.

OPERATING PRINCIPLES

Remember the best-selling book *All I Really Need to Know I Learned in Kindergarten*?[3] It highlighted how the rules of the sandbox apply to real life—rules like respect each other, don't say hurtful things, and share your toys. Over the years, I've come to appreciate that there's one thing that defines truly great teams—and that's whether they have rules of play to guide their behaviors. These "operating principles" can go a long way in minimizing team conflicts and helping people build trust and spark.

We've worked with many leaders to help them define operating principles for their management teams. Here are some examples drawn from different clients:

- We owe it to one another to communicate to each other first—good news and bad.
- We are careful not to make assumptions about each other—or our businesses.
- We focus on big issues rather than on small issues.
- We hold regular meetings, even if it's just to share information.
- We make clear the decision-making roles of the group and individuals.
- We ask challenging questions because we need to understand each other's priorities and portray each other in the best possible light.
- We don't assume that something is meant in a negative way—we check our assumptions.

- It's okay for us to say, "I don't know—I'll get back to you in twenty-four hours."
- If there are issues between us, then we first go to each other and discuss it. Only if we can't resolve it on our own will we go to our boss, and we will go together. And he'll play referee.

Whole Foods Market is an example of a company where operating principles are in force. One of its rules deals with its vendor relationships. It states that: "Employees will treat suppliers with respect, fairness and integrity, and expect the same in return. Any conflicts must be mediated and win-win solutions found. Creating and nurturing this community of stakeholders is critical to the long-term success of our company."[4]

When Whole Foods found itself in the middle of a conflict with its largest supplier of organic foods, it used this rule to ensure a successful outcome. Rather than try to impose a solution, it devoted thousands of hours to communication and mediation. The result was a new agreement that both sides hailed.

Working with the management team of a software company in California, we developed four very simple operating principles:

Rule 1: On time, on budget, no excuses.

Rule 2: Information is to be shared, not hoarded.

Rule 3: Bad news is not like wine. Share it right away.

Rule 4: Conflicts can only be resolved by communication, not triangulation.

Operating principles can take many forms. They can be short and sweet; they can be long and detailed. The important point is to take the time to define the rules for your teams. You wouldn't play a game of baseball or football without defining the rules. It's no different in the workplace.

START WITH THE RIGHT INGREDIENTS

When asked the secret of her cooking, the renowned chef Alice Waters liked to say: "Always start with the right ingredients." What's surprising is how often leaders and managers overlook this simple fact. Even one bad employee will spoil the whole bunch.

One of our clients, a financial services company, asked us to help improve the company's performance. Meeting with the management team, I was struck by the fact that one senior manager tended to foist the blame on others for the mediocre performance of his bond-trading division. When he did shoulder the blame, he did so halfheartedly, saying things like: "If I had more people, we'd be able to hit our targets," conveniently forgetting his role in setting those targets.

I talked to the CEO about the importance of having the right players on her team. She defended John, saying that he'd been a loyal and trusted confidant for years. I said, "Yes, but on a small team, one player can either elevate everyone else's game, or bring it down. Despite his loyalty, John is bringing everyone else down, and you're enabling it by not holding him accountable."

After giving this some thought, the CEO heeded my advice, and within a few months she reshuffled her management team, bringing in two new senior-level directors and reducing John's responsibilities. Six months later, when we were having coffee together, she told me: "Those were the wisest words you ever told me: that one player can elevate the whole team—or bring it down. It's incredible I had been blind to it before."

HIRING THE RIGHT PEOPLE

So how do you avoid leadership "blindness"? How do you make sure you're not confusing personal loyalty with professional competence? How do you get the right people on your team? And put them in the right roles?

One tool is "behavior-based interviewing." It's predicated on the idea that past performance is the best predictor of future achievement. The first step is to identify the precise behaviors that are most important for success in a particular job. Managing a far-flung team, turning around a business, starting a new product line, building a sales team—these might be behaviors you're looking for. Your detailed list of desired attributes becomes your litmus test—first for constructing a detailed job description and then for interviewing your candidates. During the interview process, ask for specific examples of relevant experience: "Tell me an example of how you've successfully built a sales team." "Tell me an example of how you've successfully turned around a floundering business." If the candidate can share a relevant experience, then great! If not, you've learned two things: (1) he doesn't have the necessary experience, and (2) he's not very adept at being interviewed!

TYPICAL INTERVIEW VS. BEHAVIOR-BASED INTERVIEW

TYPICAL INTERVIEW	BEHAVIOR-BASED INTERVIEW
Describe your experience in sales.	This position requires a person to make five sales calls a day while traveling in a territory from Minneapolis to Atlanta. Tell me about your experience managing those kinds of sales logistics.
Have you ever had to manage large accounts?	This position requires people to manage large accounts with three or four contacts inside the organization, all of whom need to say yes to consummate a sale. Tell me about your experience making such a sale. How did you get them all to say yes?
Describe your greatest success.	This position requires working with an internal R&D team to help them modify our product for a new launch every twelve months. Describe how you've successfully managed internal relationships with R&D teams to maximize the success of upgraded products.
What motivates you?	We expect people to be self-motivated. Describe your own motivation for success. Describe examples where you went an extra mile for a client—and for your company.
How do you handle conflicts?	Tell us how you handled a situation that made you look bad. What did you do? What did you say? What was the result?

The corollary of behavior-based interviewing is open-ended recruiting: when a position comes open, you should keep searching until you find the right person, even if it means temporarily not filling the slot. Finding the right person is simply too important to warrant settling for less.

The quest to get the right people means you should always be on the lookout for talent. After all, talented people are almost by definition not those who are pounding the pavement looking for work. So if you want to build a great company, you're going to have to employ unusual means to get the right people on board. Good leaders typically spend 25 percent of their time recruiting and developing talent. Be disciplined about whom you hire, whom you promote, and whom you reward.

It doesn't matter how big or small your organization is; the cost of settling for second best can be huge. First, there's the cost to ensure a new hire receives the proper training. That's a cost you would bear in any case. But by settling for second best, you may have to spend more time training them to make sure they don't make mistakes. Then, as you see that they require more supervision, you may spend more time checking their work. Maybe you insist on multiple sign-offs on their decisions. Maybe you revise a process to make sure their work is checked by someone every day. For the sake of filling the position, you've now added a little bit more bureaucracy to the organization.

Now comes the higher, hidden cost. The talented people in your organization start to resent the new person. They've got to deal with his or her blunders. Maybe they have to subject themselves to the same bureaucracy. This irritates them at first—then it starts to grate. Morale suffers. Ultimately, the genuinely talented people decide to move on. The net result is a significant erosion of trust—all because you failed to find the right people in the first place.

FITTING PEOPLE INTO THE RIGHT ROLE

Bob Matthews, the founder of Cable Data, one of the world's largest billing companies, was ahead of his time in thinking about how to fit people into the right roles. He had an uncanny eye for discerning what people were good at, and he wasn't afraid to put people into unfamiliar roles that would tap their hidden talents. Bob also changed people's roles regularly to see where they best fit.

"Most people aren't trained in ways that match their natural abilities," he said. "I care more about a person's natural talents than in their resumes." He hired people who'd been successful in an eclectic array of fields—a yoga instructor, a jewelry maker, a software marketer—and inserted them into leadership roles.

Bob knew that you get the most out of people when they are learning, not when they're following a routine. So every three years or so, he'd give people a new role. "I think it's important for people to get uncomfortable again," he said. "I want to continually challenge them to learn and apply their best thinking." The success of the people who worked for Bob is a testament to this vision. Several went on to lead Fortune 500 companies.

Putting people in the right roles requires courage. The CEO of one of our clients, a health-care company, elevated a talented mid-level manager to be COO, skipping over three more senior candidates. This took everyone by surprise. The COO, a woman in her mid-thirties, alleviated the concerns by asking everyone in the company: "What's the one thing we could fix that would make our business more successful—and your life here easier?" Her survey identified three priorities—which the COO focused on fixing in the first year. By checking her ego at the door and working collaboratively to get things done, she took the company where it needed to go—and built trust in the process.

VALUE PEOPLE'S TIME

There used to be a large wooden hourglass at the offices of the Public Policy Institute of California. Whenever someone came to speak during weekly all-fellows meetings, the hourglass was turned over. Why? Because the director had made a promise to his staff: "Come to these meetings to learn—and we will take no more than an hour of your time." The hourglass was his way of making good on that guarantee.

The CEO of a large bank asked me to sit in on the weekly management team meeting. The meeting had no written agenda. Each of the fourteen senior managers gave an update on the activities. The discussion veered from topic to topic. After the first thirty minutes, my attention started to flag. At the sixty-minute mark, I wondered if it would ever end. Two hours later, the meeting mercifully adjourned.

I asked the CEO if he'd ever calculated the cost of the meetings. He did a quick bit of arithmetic, and a look of amazement crossed his face: "That's fifteen thousand dollars per hour." I pointed out that he could cut his meeting time and save more than $1 million a year. He did, and his team was forever grateful.

Many companies suffer from meeting "burnout." The bandage many of them grab on to is reducing the number of meetings. But that's not smart. In a world of accelerating innovation and change, in a world where you need to lead through others, more communication is needed, not less. The key is in more crisply managed meetings. I used to have a daily management team meeting. We started at 8 a.m.; we ended at 8:30. A lot can get done in thirty minutes. Agendas can identify the key topics and decisions to be made. Information can be distributed ahead of time, reducing the need for updates. Quick emails can summarize the action steps.

HIGHLY EFFECTIVE MEETINGS

....

The key to highly effective meetings is not what you do during the meeting, but what you do before and after the meeting. Here are three of the practices that we teach:

1. **Take ownership of the agenda.** Before the meeting, decide what topics to cover, what decisions need to be made, and the time required. Send out the agenda in advance, along with any background material.

   During the meeting, remember the following mantra. "Make sure we're having the conversation we need to have." When people digress, jump in and reclaim the agenda. No one will be offended; on the contrary, people will be grateful for your leadership.

2. **Achieve closure.** Before you move on to the next item, make sure you've achieved the outcome you wanted. If an action step has been identified, make sure everyone understands. Clarify the next steps. Decide on who's going to communicate the results of the discussion. Make sure everyone is clear on their decision-making role (for more on this, see Chapter 5).

3. **Keep a written record.** You should always provide a follow-up email reminding people what was decided. This becomes a fail-safe way to check later to ensure that the necessary actions have occurred. It's invaluable for monitoring performance. Plus, you'll never have to waste people's time trying to remember what you did at the last meeting!

When he was president and CEO of General Motors in the 1930s and 1940s, Alfred Sloan had one hard-fast rule: After his meetings, he always dictated a crisp memo summarizing the results and who was going to do what. These memos became the backbone of an entire management system at GM. Sloan used them to make sure people stayed on task. He developed an elaborate system for organizing these memos, so that each project could be cross-referenced and progress could be tracked. Sloan and his senior managers used them to build accountability throughout GM. They were, in a very real sense, the key to GM's success for twenty years.

Effective meeting management is more than a discipline; it's a way of thinking about value. "How can I optimize the value of our meeting time? What can we improve next time?"[5] It may seem counterintuitive, but companies typically need more meetings—but of shorter duration.

ORIENT YOURSELF TOWARD OTHERS

Imagine you're flying on an airline with an open seating plan like Southwest. You've found yourself an aisle seat. The window and middle seats next to you are open. As people stream down the aisle looking for a place to sit, what do you do?

If you're not oriented toward other people, you sit down, put on your headphones, and bury yourself in a book. Maybe you put a section of the newspaper in the seat next to you. When someone tries to take a seat next to you, you look up briefly, scrunch up your legs, and let them fend for themselves.

But if you are oriented toward other people, you behave quite differently. You quickly make room, inviting them to take the seat next to you. You engage the person in polite conversation. You don't resent it when they have to get up to use the facilities. Instead, you get up so they can easily move to the aisle.

This "Southwest Test" may not seem like much, but it says a lot about who you are and your ability to lead through other people. A lot of information is transmitted in those few moments—am I a person who can be counted on to look out for other people? Or am I primarily looking out for myself? It goes without saying which type of person is better able to build trust—and who triggers people's cheater meters.

The book *Leadership and Self-Deception*[6] illustrates how some leaders—those who put themselves first—operate under a cloud of self-deceit. First, they deceive themselves by thinking that they can manage other people as though they were objects. Second, they delude themselves by thinking that other people won't notice their behavior. This kind of arrogance turns people off. It drives away talented people and leaves you managing a culture of mediocrity.

The authors distinguish between managers who are "in the box" and those who are "out of the box." You're in the box if you don't see how your behaviors affect others. You're out of the box if you treat other people as you would want to be treated yourself. When you lead through other people, you have their success foremost in your mind: "What does he need? How can I support her most effectively?" Often it's something that takes just a few minutes, like briefing a colleague on the outcomes from an important meeting or popping your head into your boss's office and saying: "Can I get your thinking on something?"

Every good leader is "out of the box." It's a critical part of building a high-performing organization. A corollary to this idea is leading through influence rather than authority. People who lead through influence are not afraid to invest in people who are smarter than they are, more knowledgeable than they are. Nor are they afraid to lose the argument or admit mistakes. No person can be a great leader unless he takes genuine joy in the successes of those under him. Yet many would-be leaders stumble upon this rock. They put other people down, in subtle and not-so-subtle ways. This may get you to the top—at least temporarily. But it's not leadership.

To lead by influence rather than authority doesn't mean to forgo your role and authority as a leader. But leading by influence means focusing on effective communication rather than on the bald exercise of power. It means making your case and listening carefully to opposing points of view. It means not only an open office policy but an "open mind policy." Pride of authorship isn't the issue—it's pride in results.

Sitting in Los Angeles with a group of managers of a large national chain, I was impressed how Julia, the CEO, asked each manager to express his or her goals for the company. And I was doubly impressed that her managers felt secure enough that they could offer alternative scenarios and visions for the company. Julia listened carefully and then summarized what she'd heard: "I think what we all are saying is that we want to delight our customers. That's the only vision that matters. Everything else we're talking about is just a strategy for doing that. And some of you seem to be saying that I haven't been focused enough on that."

There was a palpable look of relief on people's faces. It was clear they'd been worried. Seeing Julia listen and synthesize their visions, and hearing her commitment to the importance of customer service, enabled them to work together toward that goal—one they accomplished with flying colors over the next year.

RELIEVE THE PRESSURE

In some organizations, a relentless pressure to perform can be a drain on people's energies. Effective leaders lighten the pressure in ways that help people learn to trust one another. Psychologists call this "systemic stress management." It's why sailors get shore leave, why people get holidays, why organizations create social occasions.

At one of our clients, where hundreds of highly paid broker-dealers manage the daily ebbs and flows of the stock market, Friday afternoon get-togethers are a chance to let off steam. At the Intel campus in Roseville, California, people let off steam by taking part in volleyball games during lunch hour. Two sand courts are filled with players each day. A pickup soccer game occurs on a field nearby.

"To maintain a high level of focus is fatiguing," says Gregory Kolt, a professor of psychology at Auckland University of Technology in New Zealand. The trick, he says, is to find enough idle distractions so that you can elevate your focus at the right time.[7]

MANAGING YOUR BOSS

During a seminar I was conducting, a young manager raised his hand and asked: "This is all well and good. But how do I apply these ideas to managing my boss? How can I lead him where I think we need to go?"

I winced because of the way his question was framed. I told him that to build trust with his boss, he first needed to find a way to see the world through his boss's eyes. "You need to ask him what he's dealing with," I said. "Find out how you can help. Get him to believe you are part of the solution, not part of the problem. And then set clear expectations with your boss about what he wants from you—and what you need from him."

In "Managing Your Boss,"[8] John Gabarro and John Kotter point out that bosses "don't have unlimited time, encyclopedic knowledge or extrasensory perception; nor are they evil enemies. They have their own pressures and concerns that are sometimes at odds with the wishes of the subordinate—and often for good reason." It's up to you to find out what those concerns are and figure out how you can best support your boss.

It's important to accept that you are not going to change your boss's personality any more than you can change your own personality. At best, you might be able to suggest some small changes in behavior—but only if your boss is open to such suggestions, and only if you can show that it would benefit the entire organization. Even small changes in behavior require considerable commitment. As the old joke goes, how many psychologists does it take to change a light bulb? Only one, but the light bulb must really want to change.

SKIP MANAGEMENT

Let's talk for a moment about "skip management." That's the practice of skipping a level of management to talk to someone the next level up or down. It is easily abused and can break down trust in a hurry. At the same time, when you lead through others, you need to be able to talk to everyone.

So what are the rules around skip management? First, you should only skip a level if you inform the skipped manager about what you said and why—immediately. Second, if an important discussion occurs inadvertently (and you skipped a level), you must immediately take the time to inform the manager who was skipped. Third, if you skip a level and make a request of some kind, you have to recognize that it's just that—a request. The skipped manager has the right to review the request and make the appropriate decision within his or her delegation of authority.

A highly complex organization, with lines of authority crisscrossing each other, is ripe for mistakes of this kind. Good leaders will understand that skip management needs to take place. At the same time, they instill the habit of keeping people informed and continually building trust.

MATRIX MANAGEMENT

Matrix management is like skip management on steroids. Despite all its messy complications, matrix management is required for companies with intersecting lines of product, functional, and geographic responsibility. In this highly complex environment, with crisscrossing lines of authority, people have to be hyperaware of all the different opportunities for conflict. Good leaders make communication their number-one priority. They view the matrix as an ally through which you can get things done, not as a nuisance to avoid.

For example, the managing director of a large international bank regularly sends out weekly emails to all three thousand of the firm's senior managers, letting them know of key decisions occurring across the bank's global operations. She makes it clear that she expects them to operate as a unified organization, anticipating potential conflicts and raising them to the appropriate level of attention quickly. She routinely fields 250 responses a week where people seek clarity of direction. Her open communication policy builds trust by allowing people the freedom to communicate directly with their regional leaders.

PERFORMANCE DEVELOPMENT

Good leaders start with the right ingredients. They also give people the tools to succeed. That means giving them many opportunities to learn what they're doing well and how they can improve. It also means providing the infrastructure that encourages people to take responsibility for their own professional development.

Good leaders know the cycle of performance development. The cycle begins when a person starts working—and continues as long as the employee remains with an organization. The life cycle has these steps:

First, good leaders clearly communicate and share their expectations with their employees directly, in person. There are different levels of expectations, including those of the company,[9] those of the leader, and those of the employee. Good leaders communicate expectations in person, on an ongoing basis.

Second, they provide ongoing, timely communication and feedback about what the employee is doing well, and what areas need development. You should not wait for a formal appraisal to provide this feedback, but provide it on an ongoing basis. Depending on the quality of the employee's performance and the nature of the assignment, it may be necessary to change the employee's responsibilities and expectations. The good leader communicates this clearly, balancing appreciative and constructive feedback.

Third, on a regular basis, the leader should ask the employee to complete a self-appraisal and share it. The leader can then respond, confirming what the employee has identified and identifying the employee's specific strengths and areas needing development. Based on that discussion, the employee should create an Individual Development Plan (IDP), identifying his or her short-term development goals and long-term career goals.

The important thing to stress is that this is a positive experience. Every leader, from the CEO on down, needs to have an IDP and continuously work on their professional development. No one stops developing. It is a lifelong pursuit, and those who are actively attuned and engaged in their professional development find deep satisfaction and fulfillment.

SHARED LEADERSHIP ROLES

The issue of shared leadership is one that often snags people who are well intentioned in their efforts to lead through others. The Sierra Club tried a "troika" system with three co-equal leaders. AOL Time Warner tried to institute a system of two co-equal leaders. Both failed. The truth is that these shared arrangements don't work very well. People need clear lines of responsibility—both for those who are leading and those who are being led. People like to know who's in charge and who's making the decisions. It takes a wise leader to recognize that "shared decision making" often represents an abdication of responsibility—and a recipe for disappointment and a breakdown in trust.

One of our clients is a nonprofit organization that works to help educate urban youth. It's a small agency with twenty-five employees. It's the kind of workplace where people should be able to clearly define their roles and responsibilities. But Julie, the executive director, wanted to recognize the talents and contributions of her associate director, Morgan. So she defined her as "a partner." Morgan interpreted this to mean she would have a co-equal role in all major decisions. And, initially, this seemed to be working fine. Julie and Morgan met every morning and made many decisions by consensus.

But then things turned sour. They disagreed on a key hire. Morgan began to make decisions unilaterally about fund-raising strategy. Julie contacted me for coaching. "We spend endless time in meetings," Julie told me. She spoke of conflicts with Morgan around specific marketing practices. "I have more experience than she does. Yet she wants to argue my every suggestion."

I asked Julie how the partnering model evolved. Julie told me that Morgan had initially been hired as a consultant to help the agency define its strategic goals. Morgan had set the agency on a good direction and given it a significant lift during its start-up phase.

The question was posed: "Do you think your partnership is helping the organization work effectively now? Are you better able to achieve your goals?"

"No," Julie replied. "If anything, we're working less effectively."

"So what keeps this partnership alive?"

"I don't want to disappoint Morgan," Julie replied. "I'm afraid if I change her role, she'll leave."

"Thinking objectively, which would be better for the organization—redefining her role or her leaving?"

"Well, I guess if I look at it from that standpoint," said Julie, "we'd be better off changing her role."

I told Julie: "I think you've answered your own question. In my view, an organization needs a single person leading it. Employees need to know that a single person is in charge."

Julie understood the logic and got to work. She wrote down the new division of responsibilities, clearly stating that she would function as the chief executive and Morgan would oversee marketing. I checked in a week later and asked Julie how it was going. "Morgan was initially resistant," she said. "But I've made the change and she's on board. And the rest of the staff already seems much happier knowing whom they report to."

COACHING AND MENTORING

As part of the cycle of development, good leaders provide people coaching and mentoring. Though the terms are often used interchangeably, there is a distinct difference: a mentor typically comes from inside the organization; a coach is a professional hired from outside. Coaching is aimed at improving the performance. The work focuses on building strengths in one or two areas, such as communication, decision making, or building relationships. Typically the focus is less on technical skills, more on management skills.

One of our firm's practice areas is coaching. The process begins with the selection of a coach who is a good fit for the "coachee." The next step is a 360 assessment to gather input from the person's bosses, peers, and subordinates. That feedback is distilled into a report that the coach and coachee use to develop an Individual Development Plan (the IDP). After sharing the IDP with the person's boss, the coachee works with the coach to develop specific strategies and action steps to address areas of needed growth. For example, a manager may need to learn how to be more collaborative in decision making. Or more clear on setting expectations for subordinates. Or more effective in managing poor performers. Or better at communicating with peers. Each situation and each IDP is different.

At one of our client companies, every manager is required to get coaching. Even the CEO has a mentor. The president of a venture capital firm in San Francisco has been so impressed with the power of coaching that he uses it as one of the criteria for the companies he invests in. "I don't know a better way to ensure that a CEO perform well," he says. "Coaches help you set goals for yourself. And once you commit to those goals, a coach can keep reminding you. That's powerful feedback."

Mentoring, on the other hand, is designed to help the "mentee" or protégé learn how things are done in the organization and how to build the relationships they need to succeed. Protégés are taken under the wing of a mentor who assists them not only in developing organizational knowledge but also in facilitating a conversation about the mentee's place in the organization and possible career paths. A mentor will help you get the lay of the land in your company, understand how things work, and provide advice. A mentor is someone you can turn to for industry-specific advice and guidance—perhaps steer you toward the right business connections or the best professional association. A mentor can help you navigate treacherous waters or develop strategically important relationships.

Sometimes the relationship is informal, instigated by either the mentor or mentee. In other cases, the mentoring is a result of a formal program. For example, Intel's mentoring program is designed to ensure that all new employees learn how to succeed within the Intel culture. It began within a single team of software engineers and has now expanded to include virtually every campus. Lockheed Martin's mentoring program has only two rules. A boss can't mentor a subordinate. And there's a "no fault" divorce provision. The relationship can be terminated at any time, for any reason, by either party.

Having a mentor is important. Being a mentor is also important; it can pay big dividends in your personal and professional growth. By becoming someone's trusted advisor, you can build strong professional and personal relationships. Being a mentor is also a piece of firm ground where you can hone your mind and spirit as you embark on the more difficult climb—your own personal change.

• • •

CONCLUSION

There's a concept of community in South Africa that's called "Ubuntu." It emphasizes the interdependence of each member of the community. It recognizes a person's status as a human being, entitled to unconditional respect, dignity, value, and acceptance. But it also entails the converse.

Each person has a corresponding duty to give respect, dignity, value, and acceptance to every other member of the community.

The key to leading through others is to orient yourself toward this Ubuntu ideal—viewing other people as having needs and concerns equal to your own. When you lead through others, you make it a priority to model respectful communication. You get the right people in the right roles—and don't settle for less than the best. You lead through influence rather than authority. You take responsibility for making sure that people have the coaching and training they need to perform at their highest level. You show people that you value their time by managing meetings effectively. You develop effective teams by laying out operating principles. Ultimately, you watch the dynamics carefully, benching the players who are not meeting expectations, and giving those who are ready to play a chance at a starting role.

Theodore Roosevelt said: "The best leader is the one who has sense enough to pick good men to do what he wants done, and self-restraint enough to keep from meddling with them while they do it." When you do all these things, you build a system of trust: by placing your trust in others, they will place their trust in you.

MANAGE DECISIONS WELL

(ACV+STF+LTO+MDW+SWY) + (APC+SCF+SST+MTC+APQ) = LC

A large California nonprofit, a leader in the health-care industry, was experiencing significant problems keeping its programs within budget and within scope. No matter how hard its CEO tried, things weren't getting better. The CEO, Susan Ford, asked our firm to assess the situation. After a series of interviews and discussions, we diagnosed the problem as a lack of alignment between responsibility and accountability. The people who were ostensibly accountable—the program managers—didn't have the clear responsibility to address the problems. Too many decisions had to be kicked up the hierarchy to the CEO, delaying response time, overwhelming senior management, causing more delays and budgetary shortfalls.

We recommended that the company streamline its decision-making processes, clarifying how decisions were managed and made at every level. Our goal was to enable people closer to the front lines to make more decisions. Making the program managers both accountable *and* responsible for addressing more issues would enable the organization to be more nimble, to be more responsive to customers, and to cultivate the next generation of leaders.

Our process was straightforward: The senior leadership team, a group of five including Susan, met for several days and explored every type of decision the company made. We helped them cluster their decisions into three categories that encompassed every aspect of the company: personnel decisions, financial decisions, and program decisions. Personnel decisions included hiring, firing, compensating, and promoting. Financial decisions included budgeting, authorizing expenses, signing contracts, and ensuring collection of revenues. Program decisions included approval of program goals and specific scope (and changes in scope), okaying program and project deliverables, responding to customer concerns, and monitoring performance.

PRACTICE #4: MANAGE DECISIONS WELL

....

Decisions are the day-to-day inputs and outputs of an organization. To build trust, leaders must build systems that result in good decisions being made throughout the organization. They need to teach people how to manage decisions effectively—to design a decision process. They need to reframe how difficult decisions are communicated and made. Delegations must be clear. Otherwise, the sludge of bureaucracy creeps in and paralyzes the organization. Most important, people must shift their orientation to making and *managing* their decisions.

Obviously this was a big task. Our job was to keep the process on track and make sure the team successfully dealt with each of these categories without burning out. In each case, we first asked: Is this the CEO's decision to manage and make, meaning Susan manages the process, consults with others, and makes the decision? Or is this a delegated decision, meaning Susan delegates the authority to manage and make the decision to someone else.

As we did the first pass through these three categories, the management team had its first "aha" moment. Too many decisions were Susan's to manage and make. For example, she was ultimately deciding *on every new hire* in the organization. This "aha" moment helped Susan appreciate how much decision authority she needed and wanted to delegate downward.

The second question we asked was: If it's delegated, what do we mean by that? What authority is Susan actually delegating? Using a tool that

I'll describe in detail later in this chapter, the team defined three types of delegated decisions. As it clarified the authority, the team also identified where obsolete job descriptions conflicted with these new delegations. For example, the medical director's role needed to be redefined so that he didn't act as a choke point over certain program decisions.

At the conclusion, the senior team had a three-page matrix that defined who made what decisions. As team members looked it over, they marveled at what they had done. "We've brought more clarity to our work than we've ever had before," the COO said. "This is going to blow people's minds," a senior program officer remarked, "when people see how much trust Susan is placing in us."

The results over the next year were profound. The eight program leaders stepped up and exerted more leadership and management over the myriad projects under their wings. Budget variances stopped occurring because they were detected and managed much earlier. New provider contracts were signed because program leaders were taking ownership for marketing. The senior leadership team became more strategic and focused. The organization had found by managing decisions well, it had generated greater levels of trust—and spark.

• • •

I'm always amazed when people use job descriptions to define decision-making roles and responsibilities. Without being clear about the actual decision-making authority, a job description simply isn't sufficient. The fuzziness in roles leads to unnecessary conflicts and turf battles, as illustrated in the following case study.

After a frustrating meeting, Carly, the senior vice president of a large US-based bank, took aside one of her senior managers. "Dave, our telemarketing folks are calling on the same customers as our direct mail folks. We've got product offers going out in five different formats with different terms listed. Customers are confused. Let's do what it takes to fix this."

Dave took Carly's directive to mean he had the responsibility for solving the problem. He was the senior product manager overseeing small business lines. He gave Carly the high sign. "I'll get it under control," he told her.

Dave gathered the relevant product supervisors together for a planning session. He helped them chart out the various products and market channels. He assembled a team to analyze the five-year performance of each product and channel. Dave then asked the team to segment the market intelligently and identify the areas where the bank could most quickly achieve higher levels of profitability.

It became clear to Dave's team that equity lines of credit for small business owners were an important target of opportunity. The bank was offering five different products, each with its own terms and conditions. "We need to narrow our offerings down to three, with each channel supporting all three options," Dave told the group. "I want to see an implementation plan in a week's time. Get to work on it immediately. If you have any questions, please call me."

Each day, Dave checked in with the various members of the team, asking for a progress report. Each day he was surprised to find that people were falling behind the deadline. He called another meeting. Two of the team members failed to show. "What gives?" he asked. "Why aren't we getting this done?"

Silence prevailed for a moment. Then one of the product managers spoke. "We're not sure you have authority to do this. Doesn't Carly have to give it the green light? It's her division, after all."

"Carly has delegated this decision to me," said Dave. "I'm consulting with her, of course. But it's my responsibility to develop this plan."

At that moment, Carly happened to pass by. Dave waved and asked her to join the meeting. "There's some question about what you've asked for in regards to the small business market," he said. "Could you give me two minutes and clarify it for us?"

Carly paused and said: "I want your ideas on how to fix all the problems in that area. We've got a senior management meeting in Chicago in two weeks, and it's one of the topics on the agenda. I want your ideas to be involved before I make the final call."

The product managers all looked at one another. There was an awkward silence.

Dave looked at Carly. "We've got to talk right now," he said. "Meeting's adjourned."

A story like this highlights how important it is to be clear about decision-making roles and responsibilities. Needless to say, Dave felt chopped off at the knees. He and Carly eventually repaired the damage. But the incident put a dent in Dave's reputation—and highlighted the lack of good communication at the bank.

What could Carly or Dave have done differently? Dave could have followed the basic rule to ask questions and clarify decision-making roles and responsibilities. But Carly was also confusing and ambiguous in her choice of words: "Fix this" implied a delegation of responsibility to Dave to take action. So some of the blame falls on her. Carly's communication needed to be clarified, and it was Dave's job to do so. Rather than charge out the door, Dave needed to sit down with Carly and say: "Okay, what exactly does that mean? What is my role in this decision? Are you delegating the authority to decide to me? Or merely asking for a recommendation?" Until he had gotten answers to these questions, he shouldn't have left her office.

DECISIONS: THE HEART AND SOUL OF THE ORGANIZATION

Decisions are the atoms of every organization. Every new product launched, every new service offered, every process made more efficient and reliable is a result of hundreds of decisions. Effective leaders view their worlds through this lens, rather than through the lens of hierarchies, org charts, or chains of command. To build high levels of trust, teamwork, and innovation, effective managers focus on clarifying decision-making responsibilities. (Note that I didn't say "roles and responsibilities," which is a common mistake.) Once you know the decision-making responsibilities, you've defined the role.

Effective leaders and managers are constantly on the lookout for opportunities to clarify decision-making authority. This means difficult conversations often need to occur. First of all, it means clarifying for people their precise decision-making role, which sometimes translates into less responsibility than they think they have. The manager of a large publishing company asked me to lunch one day and said: "I need help learning how to be a better leader. What do you see as the most important thing I need to do?" Without missing a beat, I replied: "Be clear about delegation. Which decisions do you want to make? Which are you delegating to others? You can't be afraid to have those discussions."

Our research shows few leaders pay much attention to *managing* decisions. They don't know the appropriate vocabulary—for example, they confuse collaboration with consensus. They fail to design decision processes with the right sequence of goal setting, data collection, input gathering, stakeholder engagement, and brainstorming. As a result, they fail to leverage themselves as leaders. Either they go too far or not far enough in empowering others. They fail to achieve the optimum balance of engagement and efficiency in making the decision.

THE FIVE TYPES OF DECISIONS

Let's begin with one of the most important tools of successful decision management—understanding the five types of decision processes: autocratic, consultative, consensus, delegated, and democratic. Each implies dramatically different roles for the people involved.

AUTOCRATIC DECISIONS

The easiest type of decision is autocratic: it's a decision you make yourself. You pick out your shirt in the morning. You respond to your email. No one else gets involved. There are two subtypes:

- You make the decision by yourself using the information you have available.
- You obtain information from another person (or other people), and then decide by yourself.

If you reflect on all the decisions you make during a day, you can appreciate how much of life is filled with autocratic decisions. But they are also relatively trivial. What you eat for breakfast, where you park your car, how you organize your desk—these are decisions you make on your own.

I can only think of three situations in which a leader or manager should make important company decisions in this manner: (1) when the decision is straightforward and you have all the information necessary, in which case you still need to communicate what you've decided and why; (2) when the pressure of the clock forces you to make the decision quickly—in which case you need to explain those circumstances to people who are affected; or (3) when there's an overarching importance to maintaining secrecy.

Leaders who want to build an organization operating with high levels of trust and spark should not make important decisions autocratically. Instead, they need to use one of the other four processes.

CONSULTATIVE DECISIONS

A consultative decision means you recognize that you don't have all the information you need and you want to actively engage other people in the process. You literally consult with another person or persons. At the same time, you make it clear that the final call is yours—it is most definitely not a consensus decision (more on that in a moment).

Again, there are two subtypes:

- You involve other people individually by sharing the issues and obtaining their data, ideas, and recommendations. Then you decide.

- You involve other people as a team or a group by sharing the issues and obtaining data, generating ideas, and developing recommendations. In other words, it is a highly collaborative process. But it is not consensus—it's clear from the outset that you have the final say.

Who should be consulted in a consultative decision? The ground rule is this: if someone's going to be deeply affected by the decision, or if someone has relevant facts or expertise, then his or her input is important. That doesn't mean you have to engage everyone—or consult with every expert. But you do need to cast a wide net. The best decisions are made when you hear different points of view and debate a variety of recommendations, even if you have to stretch farther than you might like.

When the consultative process is managed well, it's clear who is going to make the decision. "Ultimately the call will be mine," you'd say. "But we need to hear everyone's views in order for me to make the best decision."

There are certain phrases you want to avoid. Don't say: "We need to agree on this," or "I want to get your buy-in." This implies a different type of decision—a consensus decision. This lack of clarity chips away at trust and teamwork. People think to themselves: "You misled me into thinking that I have a larger role to play than I actually do." Avoid this trap at all costs!

So in answer to the question, "What's my role in this decision?" the leader of a consultative decision should say: "Your role is to bring to the table the relevant information and ideas you have. Your viewpoint is important because this decision will affect you. In the end, because this is a decision for which I am responsible. I need to make the call. And if I make the wrong decision, I assume full responsibility."

CONSENSUS DECISIONS

A consensus decision is a group decision. In general, it means that the vast majority of the group supports a particular course of action, and no one in the group is opposed to it. Consensus involves a lengthy process of sharing data, brainstorming options, and thoroughly airing all relevant information and viewpoints. It requires that the group be deliberate in managing the decision process collectively—if someone feels the process is unfair, the group needs to stop and take stock and repair the process so that no one feels left out.

Again, there are two subtypes:

- You and another individual share the issues, and then you both generate and evaluate alternatives and reach a decision that you mutually agree on.
- A larger group shares the issues, collects data, generates options, evaluates alternatives, and reaches a decision.

A consensus decision requires extensive attention to process. The group has to meet often enough to hear all the evidence and viewpoints. Someone has to facilitate the process—to organize the meetings, keep the group focused, record the results of each meeting, and summarize the progress made. Perhaps the role of facilitator rotates among members of the group. Perhaps a professional facilitator is brought in. A team may spend several weeks reaching consensus on a particular decision—or even longer!

CONSULTATION VS. CONSENSUS

To build high levels of trust, people in leadership roles need to engage other people in making decisions. They need to demonstrate a willingness to listen, to take other points of view seriously, and to explain their own point of view.

Ultimately, however, a leader needs to be clear about which decisions lie within his or her authority. These decisions should be made consultatively, not by consensus. You can use a process of "deep consultation," in which people have plenty of time to discuss, dream, and deliver their input. In essence, the process of "deep consultation" means engaging people in a process to understand the current reality, brainstorm options, and recommend what to do.

But deep consultation doesn't equal consensus. Nor does collaboration or teamwork equal consensus. On high-performing teams, people know their roles and work collaboratively together, sharing information and ideas, but not everyone on the team is equal. There's a leader vested with the responsibility to make the final call.

There are situations where consensus is unavoidable. A group of people representing different organizations may need to operate by consensus. A board of directors may operate by consensus to the extent it can. (Otherwise it must operate democratically.) But when a leader misleads people into thinking they have a larger role than they do, it erodes trust. At some point, the faux consensus will be revealed for what it is—a pretense. Once trust is broken, it is very difficult to repair.

Because consensus decisions consume more time and resources than other types of decisions, they should be reserved for two specific occasions: First, when the stakes are high and the responsibility for making the decision and owning the results needs to be shared. Second, when a group of peers is working to reach agreement and no one has final authority.

Too often, managers use consensus to make decisions that should be made consultatively. This erodes trust. People want their leaders to assume responsibility. They don't want to try to reach consensus if someone has the authority to decide. But this is what happens every day, in organizations around the world. I vividly remember the head of information technology for a New York bank trying to facilitate consensus among her group of two hundred employees. The issue was the selection of a new suburban location for the bank's back office. She attempted to engage her employees in a discussion of whether to move to Long Island or New Jersey. Yet the decision had already been made by her boss, and it was clear to her employees that her hands were tied. The faux process quickly turned ugly. As a result, there was an open revolt against her leadership.

The lesson is clear: People respect leaders who take responsibility for making a decision consultatively. You just have to be clear at the outset about how the decision will be made. The clearer you are in managing decisions, the more effective you will be at leveraging yourself as a leader.

DELEGATED DECISIONS

The delegated decision also has two subtypes:

- You determine that another individual has the judgment necessary to make the decision, so you delegate it and in so doing acknowledge that you will accept and support the decision he or she makes. This makes it a delegated consultative decision. (As someone who's affected, you should be consulted before the decision is made—but you recognize that your point of view may not prevail.)

- You determine that a team or group has the judgment to make the decision, so you delegate it to the group and accept and support the decision the group makes. This makes it a delegated consensus decision. (Again, you may be consulted, but your opinion may not carry the day.)

Most managers think they know what it means to delegate. But let's be clear. When we delegate a decision to someone else, we are giving that person (or that team) the authority to make the decision. We're not holding back a trump card. If we do, it's a faux delegation. If you delegate the decision, then you trust the other person to make the decision—and you are going to support it in most cases (see below).

But that's not all there is to it. Delegated decisions are also consultative. In other words, when you delegate the authority to someone else to make the decision, you expect that person to consult with those who'll be affected by the decision—including you—before they make the call. That's a fundamental rule of delegation that bears repeating again and again: in a delegated process, you still consult with those from whom you received the delegation.

When you delegate a decision, an effective manager will support the decision that is made—and not overrule it. If the "delegate" selects a different option from the one you favored, you still have to support his or her decision. Assuming, that is, that you want to build trust. Otherwise, it's a faux delegation.

A faux delegation can undermine morale just as insidiously as faux consensus. Telling someone to handle a business decision and then stepping in to reverse it will tear down trust. Delegation requires that you respect someone's ability to make the right decision. If the delegate exercises poor judgment, you (and he) will just have to live with the error—and learn from it.

At the start of this chapter, I talked about the tool we used with Susan and her leadership team to clarify three types of delegated authorities. This is how it works:

- **Level A:** You are delegated the authority to initiate the decision, gather input, collect the necessary data, generate options, and make a recommendation. The ultimate decision is still made by your boss. Once the decision is made, it's your job to communicate what was decided and why.
- **Level B:** You are delegated all the authority in Level A, plus you are delegated the authority to make the decision. You also must notify your boss of the decision.
- **Level C:** You are delegated all the authority in Level B, plus there's no expectation that you notify your boss.

Using this three-level tool, you can gain clarity quickly on who's responsible for managing which delegated decisions—and how the communication needs to flow. Note that in a typical hierarchy, there's a waterfall of these delegations. At each level of the hierarchy, the level of delegation is likely to change. To build trust, you need to clarify the delegations all the way down to the first-level supervisors.

DEMOCRATIC DECISIONS

In some instances a decision is decided by vote. These are democratic decisions, and they also have two subtypes:

- A group of people working together gathers information, discusses alternatives, and then makes a decision by vote. This is typical of an elected body, such as a city council.

- A group of people largely unknown to one another gathers information and then makes a decision by vote. This is typical of a group of citizens in a democracy.

A democratic decision requires an orderly process that is well understood by all potential voters. The voting rules need to be clear well ahead of the vote. Who is eligible? How will the vote be taken? How will it be tallied? What constitutes "winning"—is it a majority, two-thirds, 55 percent, or some weighted voting system? If the eligible voters are members of a board, owners of a company, or citizens in a democracy, the organization has an obligation to communicate the terms of the upcoming vote. These issues are typically worked out well in advance of any democratic decision and incorporated into the policies of the organization.

Most democratic decisions are straightforward, because there are clear rules in place for when to use a voting process. But there are exceptions. I remember working with a bank where every senior manager got to vote on each and every goal and objective in the strategic plan. If it got a majority of votes, it went in the plan. If not, it didn't. When I pointed out that the test of a good strategy wasn't whether it was popular but whether it was effective, I was told: "This is just the way we do things here." I had to smile a little when I read two years later that the company had filed for bankruptcy.

DECISION MAPS

Complex decisions are typically "nested"—meaning that several different types of decision processes feed into one final decision. It's like a set of wooden Russian dolls that slip neatly one inside the other. In deciding to purchase a new IT system, for example, a team may be *delegated* responsibility to reach *consensus* on a recommendation to forward to the senior management team, where the decision will be made *consultatively* by the CEO, who will in turn take the plan to the board for a final, ratifying, *democratic* vote.

To manage the decision well, this process needs to be well understood by everyone. By being transparent about the process, you can help people behave more effectively and efficiently. In the example above, the team of engineers may figure that it doesn't need to spend time reaching consensus on a single option, knowing that the final decision will be up to the CEO and the board. Rather, it can reach consensus on the two best options and forward those for their consideration.

Let's look now at how you can use a "decision map" to clarify a nested decision. Consider the decision to open a new store in an international chain like Starbucks. A location scout is *delegated* responsibility for identifying potential new locations. The scout forwards these potential locations to a regional manager. The regional manager *delegates* to a planning team the job of studying these potential locations and developing business plans for sites the team thinks are worth pursuing.

This team is composed of three people. A market analyst determines sales projections. A budget analyst prepares a budget for the location, showing both projected revenues and costs, including labor, rent, equipment costs, etc. A financial analyst develops a financing and ownership plan for the store.

Each member of the team takes responsibility for his or her area. As individuals, they *consult* with their team. They can reject the scouts' sites or pursue them. The team is directed to reach *consensus* on any recommendation to open a new store. The team develops a business plan that includes all the information related to projected sales revenues, costs (both capital and operating), plus an ownership and financing plan.

SAMPLE DECISION MAP

1. SCOUT	2. PLAN	3. REVIEW	4. APPROVE
• Starbucks "scout" identifies potential new locations. • Scout forwards to regional manager.	• Regional manager delegates to team. • Team develops plan. • Team forwards plan to regional manager.	• Regional manager reviews plan, makes changes. • Regional manager informs team. • Regional manager forwards plan to VP.	• Vice president approves (or disapproves). • VP delegates to regional manager to implement.
Scout consults with regional manager.	Manager delegates to team; team reaches consensus; team consults with regional manager.	Regional manager informs team; manager consults with vice president.	Vice president delegates to regional manager.

Once its recommendation is complete, the team forwards the business plan to the regional manager for her to review and approve (or disapprove). At that point in the process, the team plays a *consultative* role. Once the regional manager approves the plan, she forwards it to the regional vice president for a final decision. That's another *consultative* decision. When he's approved the plan, the decision is complete and the process is complete.

Decision maps are a powerful tool. Every nested decision can be depicted visually so that people can grasp the multiple steps in the process and their particular role in it. Sometimes the same person may wear two hats: one as a team member, another as a boss. Clarifying the decision process—and continuing to manage the communication during the decision—is the essence of managing decisions well.

Defining the roles of external stakeholders in a decision is also important. By using a decision map, you can build trust by managing people's expectations. In many of our planning processes, we gather input from stakeholders at the beginning of the process and then bring a draft plan to stakeholders for further input before it is finalized. They reciprocate by taking more responsibility for their part of the process.

CLARIFY EXPECTATIONS

Leaders and managers who want to build high levels of trust as they delegate need to clarify expectations. If you have a very specific outcome in mind, make sure you communicate it. Don't expect people to develop telepathic powers! If you have a particular expectation in terms of how a report will look, provide an example. If you know the data you want, explain what it is. You shouldn't expect people to understand intuitively what you want unless you've worked with them for many years.

Part of laying out expectations is defining a timetable. It's not fair to leave people guessing whether something is due next week or next month. You should also identify the critical path decisions (that is, decisions upon which other decisions are contingent and dependent). For example, in opening a new store, the construction schedule will affect hiring, promotions, acquiring inventory, and so forth. Sharing the timetables for critical path issues and sharing updates of those timetables will build trust. You may worry that you're micromanaging. But you're not. You're doing what's necessary to ensure alignment of expectations and strong levels of trust.

A key part of clarifying expectations is giving people context so they understand why a given decision is important. Why are we focusing on this customer segment now? Or this location? Or this particular timing? As a middle manager for a large retail chain told me: "My job is to communicate the rationales for our decisions, enlarge understanding, and provide light through the trees."

As you start to manage decisions well, delegate decisions downward, and clarify expectations, you move away from a hierarchical culture and begin building a leadership culture, where people focus on the overall goal and their role in achieving it. The "we/they" distinction disappears. What emerges is a culture in which people act both like leaders and followers simultaneously. This cultural progression is shown on the following page.

STAGES OF ORGANIZATIONAL CULTURE

STAGE 1: THE HIERARCHICAL CULTURE	A culture in which decisions are made by a boss or series of bosses. Communication, for the most part, is one-way, top to bottom.
STAGE 2: THE GOAL-DRIVEN CULTURE	A culture in which people are encouraged to achieve common goals. Communication is more dynamic, because goals are being articulated and tied to performance measures.
STAGE 3: THE VALUES-BASED CULTURE	A culture in which people make decisions based on shared understanding of what is essential to the company's success and related performance information. Communication is complex, because people are empowered to make decisions.
STAGE 4: THE LEADERSHIP CULTURE	A culture in which the "we/they" dichotomy dissolves, and everyone is united in a seamless system of communication and performance. Communication is highly complex, because everyone feels empowered to lead and follow simultaneously.

MANAGING CONFLICT

Part of managing decisions well is learning how to manage conflicts effectively. There are two types of conflict. One reflects differences in priorities, approaches, and ways of seeing things. This kind of conflict is natural, since it typically reflects different viewpoints, historical perspectives, roles in the organization, or different styles. Helping people figure out how to navigate these kinds of conflicts will build trust. It will also ensure the best decisions get made, through the natural give and take that reflects different people's views.

The second type of conflict stems from past breaches of trust. It's reflected in jealousy, resentment, and a refusal to work with other people. It is also natural. But it sucks up people's time and distracts them from getting things done.

FLAWLESS DECISIONS

....

During one of my workshops on decision making, the head of a large heath-care system asked me: "Don't you have some simple formula for flawless de-cision making, even for tough decisions?" I thought about it for a moment and wrote down three things on a flipchart:

1. Spell it out
2. Follow through
3. Communicate the results

Over time, I refined this list, adding details to each step.

Step 1. Spell It Out
- Define the desired results
- Define the process, step by step
- Clarify decision-making roles at each step
- Write down expectations, including timetable
- Identify critical path issues

Step 2. Follow Through
- Monitor progress
- Keep people informed
- Address conflicts
- Adhere to the decision process

Step 3. Communicate the Results
- Communicate the decision
- Explain the rationales
- Provide feedback on process and results
- Recognize people for their contribution

To build high levels of trust, you need to establish clear ground rules for dealing with both types of conflict. Here's what I would say: "Conflict over points of view is expected. Until the decision is made, I expect there to be disagreements among you. You need to talk to each other directly and understand each other's point of view. It's important that you talk about your underlying assumptions and find out what data you agree on, and where you disagree. Above all, don't ask someone else to referee your conflict. Learn to work it out yourselves. Only ask for a referee after you've exhausted all efforts to figure this out on your own."

Make sure you also include this ground rule: "Once the decision is made, then the time for debate is over. We will all stand united behind the decision."

For dealing with the second type of conflict, I would set this ground rule: "You will experience disagreements of a personal nature. It is inevitable. You may find that you simply do not like another person, or you may find that you resent things they've done in the past. Although these types of conflicts will occur, you cannot let them affect your performance. If they do affect your work, you need to take responsibility for figuring out a strategy to stop that from happening. If you let it continue to affect your work, then this is not the organization for you."

Real trust only comes after people have been through a few battles together. It's the leader's job to make sure ground rules are in place. When the rules of engagement are clear, fair, and consistently applied, then the battles can be fun, rather than debilitating.

Here's another example of operating principles related to decision making. These were developed by the CEO of a financial services company:

1. Loyalty means giving me your honest opinion, whether you think that I will like it or not. Disagreement in the early stages stimulates me. But once the decision is made, the debate ends. From that point on, loyalty means executing that decision as though it were your own.

2. In a crisis, don't be stampeded by first reports. Don't let your judgment run ahead of the facts. And when the facts do show up, question them if they don't add up. Something deeper and wiser than bits of data informs our instincts.

3. Bad news is not wine. It does not improve with age. If you do not want me to jump in and you can still handle it, I will not. But I never want to find out when it is too late for me to make a difference.

4. Don't ever leave my office uncertain as to what I mean. If you keep asking me, I will assume there is something wrong with my transmitter, not your receiver. Once you leave, however, the responsibility rests 100 percent with you.

5. If there are issues between team members, then first go to each other and try to resolve them together. Don't come to me in the third round of a fifteen-round fight. Only if you can't resolve it on your own come to me, and come together. And I'll play referee.

6. Never let your ego get so close to your arguing position that when your position goes down, your ego goes with it.

7. Always check the small things. Never neglect details, even to the point of being a pest.

8. Occasionally you need to stand up and fight. But don't make enemies. Opponents are okay. But today's enemy may be needed as tomorrow's friend.

The fact that this CEO took the time to spell out and discuss these principles is a sign of good leadership. That he talks about these principles regularly and cements them with the members of his team is a sign that he's very intent on building trust.

We've worked with dozens of leaders and management teams to develop similar operating principles. Who's going to be involved on which decisions? Which leaders need to meet regularly, and how often? How often do we revisit the delegations of responsibility? People work more effectively together once they start talking about *how* they want to work together. Trust builds naturally when the expectations are clear. What's surprising is that so many people never have this kind of conversation in the first place.

DECISION MAKING IN MATRIXED ORGANIZATIONS

In matrixed organizations, where the crisscrossing lines of product and functional and regional responsibility make it impossible to assign responsibility to any one person, consensus decision making is the norm.

Functional titles, like VP of marketing or head of finance, may make it sound like one person has responsibility for all things related to marketing or finance. But intersecting these functional responsibilities are product managers who act as CEOs of particular product lines, along with teams of people who are responsible for implementation.

Needless to say, the rules I laid out earlier for making consensus decisions apply in matrixed organizations. A key lies in identifying these nodes where consensus needs to occur regularly, and developing a system of communication that can function smoothly and efficiently. For example, in working with a large bank with offices in every time zone, we developed protocols for how often the decision makers at these nodes would talk (no less than once a week) and a formal set of operating principles for managing and communicating decisions to the bank's regional and functional leaders.

By the way, anxiety about decision-making authority results in most of the background distrust in an organization. Power is status. Authority is status. Where people are oriented around functional roles and authority, there is lots of noise—lots of withholding of information resulting in lots of back-channel sources of information and gossip and distrust.

To build trust, effective leaders keep the noise in check by focusing people on making good decisions. They focus on communicating the process, and they organize people around decisions rather than authority. They arm their employees with the tools to communicate effectively amid the intersecting layers of authority and responsibility—and to address conflicts when they occur.

MANAGING TOUGH DECISIONS

Managers and leaders often have to make tough "right vs. right" decisions where there are strong arguments on both sides. Should a new product be cancelled or redesigned? Should a factory be closed or retooled? Should people be fired or retrained? Ultimately the toughest decisions create winners and losers. In the toughest kinds of decisions, you stand to lose yourself.

Here are a few insights I've gleaned over the years into managing these kinds of decisions.

We make trade-offs every day. We go to the office early rather than go to the gym. We stay late rather than come home early to play with the kids. We make these kinds of decisions often—often unconscious of their impact. We view the immediate trade-off as negligible, even though their cumulative impact can be life altering.

It's only when someone confronts us that we ask: "Why don't I spend more time with the family?" "Why don't I spend more time exercising?" Then the trade-offs suddenly look large. When we open our eyes to all the alternatives we forgo, suddenly the most mundane decision seems highly important. What's the lesson? That every decision requires giving up some potential benefits. You can't have it all. So don't beat yourself up about it.

Second, the more data-centric you are in your decision making, the easier it will be to make tough decisions. Invite other people's perspectives. Listen to what they have to say. Gather the relevant data early in the decision-making process. Even if it seems like a chore, you'll benefit from what you learn. Ask people to challenge your assumptions. As you will learn later in this chapter, it is our assumption of competence that is often the biggest barrier to making the best decision. The human mind becomes far better at making decisions when it balances emotional and rational intelligence. If your heart is telling you to follow a particular course, gather some facts first to see if it's really the best option.

Third, use the 80–20 rule. If you have 80 percent confidence in a particular option, then go with it.[1] It takes too long to get the final 20 percent. The loss of time is critical in today's business environment. Indecision is deadly. It's far better to move forward than to risk standing still.

Finally, don't be afraid to reverse course. Taking risks and being wrong is part of leadership. Great leaders recognize when they've made a wrong choice, admit it openly, and change direction quickly. In the process, they don't punish themselves or other people for what went wrong. Instead, they look to the future and celebrate the company's willingness to adapt.

THE GROW MODEL

Tough decisions need to be organized so that people can move through them in a logical way. One technique to help people manage difficult discussions is the GROW model.[2] It's a tool facilitators use to manage virtually any kind of tough conversation. It works like this.

The *G* in GROW stands for "goal." The first thing in a difficult conversation is to establish the goal of the discussion—and the overall goal you're trying to achieve. Maybe it's to clear the air. Or define the next step in a decision. Or to fix a problem. Or address a looming competitor. Talking about the goal first ensures people are oriented toward the same goal. As an example, let's assume the goal is to fix a database so that people can enter data more easily from different locations.

The *R* in GROW stands for "reality." The second thing people need to talk about is the current reality. What's going on? How did we get here? What do we know? What don't we know? Using the database example, the current reality may be that people aren't using the same fields consistently, records are inaccurate, and the database can't import data from other sources.

The *O* in GROW stands for "options." What could you do to fix the database? Hire a contractor? Change the management? Establish tighter procedures? Set priorities for what gets fixed first? Scrap the existing platform? Here's where people need to engage in brainstorming and share their ideas.

Finally, the *W* in GROW stands for "will"—as in, what will we do? This is the time for people to decide on the next step. It can be the toughest part of the discussion, since a decision means forgoing other options. Perhaps the decision is to hire a contractor to deliver an objective assessment of the database. Then that's what will happen.

Teaching people the GROW model helps them feel more confident and comfortable in managing tough conversations. And that's a key part of managing decisions well.

THE GROW MODEL

FACTOR	QUESTIONS TO ASK
Goal	• What is the issue you want to tackle? • In the long term, what is your goal related to this issue? What is the time frame? • What intermediate steps can you identify, with their time frames?
Reality	• What is the present situation in more detail? • What and how great is your concern about it? • Who is affected by this issue? • How much control do you personally have over the outcome?
Options	• What are all the different ways you could approach this issue? • What else could you do? • What would you do if you had more time or a larger budget, or if you were the boss? • What would you do if you could start again with a clean slate, with a new team?
Will	• What option or options do you choose? • What are your next steps? • To what extent does this meet all your objectives? • What could arise to hinder you in taking these steps?

COMMUNICATE THE RESULTS

At some point, the decision is made. The next step is telling people the results and explaining the rationales behind the decision. Surprisingly, this is where a lot of decision processes break down. You may be done, but others are still in the dark. A complex decision affects a lot of people. I've never seen an instance in which people erred in communicating a decision too broadly. On the other hand, I've seen countless examples of failing to let key people know what happened.

Once the decision is made, you should convene the people involved and ask for their feedback on how well the decision was managed. What worked well? And how could it be better managed the next time? This feedback may seem unnecessary—but believe me, you will glean things that can help you improve all your future decision processes. Don't forget to publicly recognize the people involved. Small tokens of appreciation—a team T-shirt, a team photo—are important symbols of having participated in an important decision. Small things can symbolize big contributions and provide people the recognition that builds trust.

THE POINT OF RESOLVE

....

"The point of resolve" is the moment when an individual or a group summons up the will to make a tough decision. There is risk of loss—and the opportunity for substantial reward. But at some point the door opens, you make the decision, and suddenly it's behind you. Ahead of you are the consequences. But for the moment, you are at the point of resolve.

When we make tough decisions, hundreds of factors and points of argument come into play. The swirl can confuse us. The process can feel out of control. But at some point, we reach a point of resolve. Once you break through, you're past the moment of resolve and into implementation mode. There's no turning back.

To be an effective leader, you need to tell people about these moments of resolve. People need to know you've made a tough decision, that you've committed to a course of action, and that there's no turning back. People look for signs of resolve in their leaders—it builds trust to know that their leaders are willing to make tough stands.

Once the decision is made, there's a critical ground rule that comes into play: everyone needs to stand united in supporting the decision, even if you opposed it earlier. Leaders who want to build trust enforce this ground rule and make no exceptions.

DECISION-MAKING STYLES

Adding to the rich stew of decision making is the fact that we each have our own preferred style of decision making. Each style is prone to certain habits in making decisions. Knowing your style, and being aware of the pitfalls of each style, is an important step in becoming a leader—and helping build the skills of the people around you.

The Straight Talk® system of communication styles[3] that I developed in 1995 can give you insights into your preferred style of decision making.

Each of the four primary styles favors a certain approach to making decisions. Here's a brief preview of the four: Directors, Expressers, Thinkers, and Harmonizers.

Director: Directors are hard-charging, action-oriented leaders, focused on results. The Director's style of communicating is assertive and task oriented. Directors operate on the assumption that quick action and decisiveness are valued, and that people are rewarded for getting things done, the sooner the better. Directors frame the world as a competitive place of action and decisiveness.

Expresser: Expressers focus on leading through their creative ideas. The Expresser's style of communicating is assertive and people oriented. Their operating assumption is that people should feel free to voice their opinions, think outside of the box, and articulate what they feel. They like to entertain. Expressers frame the world as a place where people are recognized for their personal creativity and achievement.

Thinker: Thinkers are detail-oriented leaders and focused on what it takes to get the job done right. The Thinker's communication style is less assertive than the Director and Expresser. Like Directors, Thinkers are also task oriented; they assume that there's a best way to do things—and it's their job to make sure no mistakes are made. They feel rewarded when a task or project is done well. They frame the world as a place in which to solve problems and get things done.

Harmonizer: Harmonizers lead by supporting others. Their communication style is also less assertive than the Director and Expresser. Like Expressers, Harmonizers are people oriented. They operate on the assumption that they need to look after the needs of the team and other people's welfare. They feel rewarded when the team performs well. They frame the world as a place where relationships with people are the most important aspect of life and prefer to work collaboratively.

Each of these styles prefers to make decisions a certain way. Let's start with Directors. They like to make decisions quickly. They aren't afraid to take risks. They tend to see the big picture rather than the details, so they like making long-term decisions.

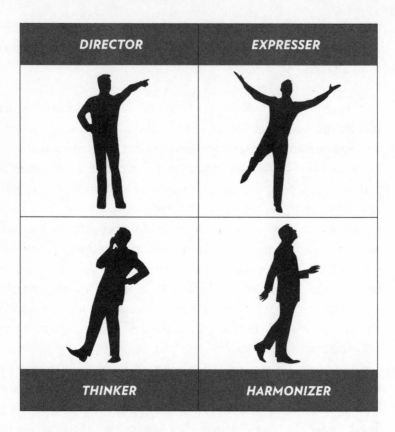

Expressers like to brainstorm. They're outgoing and creative. They don't mind taking risks. They tend to think "out of the box" more than others might like.

Thinkers focus on details. They prefer to make decisions carefully, after considering all the implications of each option. They like to focus on solving one problem at a time and consider each step logically, making lists of exactly what needs to be done.

Harmonizers like to do what's good for the team or group. Harmonizers don't like to rock the boat or upset the status quo. They want to fix the problem, but do it in such a way that no one's feelings get hurt.

Naturally, each of these styles prefers certain *kinds* of decision. Directors like decisions that focus on big strategic issues. Thinkers like to solve problems. Expressers like brainstorming. Harmonizers like decisions that focus on helping people work together better.

Understanding each of these styles will help you manage decisions well. For example, in any kind of decision-making process, it helps to have a balance of all four styles. Too many Directors and Expressers in a room can result in a lot of loud voices and conflict. Too many Thinkers and Harmonizers in the room can result in analysis paralysis. As in anything, the art lies in finding the proper mix and balance.

Taking it to the next level, each individual should become aware of his or her style and learn how to flex that style according to the situation. I'm not talking about behaving in a way that's uncomfortable for you. But if a Director can exercise more patience, if an Expresser can listen more, if a Thinker can be more open to hearing out of the box options, and if the Harmonizer can be more open to change, this is a major step toward building trust.

THE ASSUMPTION OF COMPETENCE

Human beings are a paradox. We can ponder the subtlest questions, like the origins of matter or the beginning of time. We pride ourselves on the quality of our intellects. But at the same time we are hardwired to make assumptions that can make us look downright dumb.

Psychologists have long known that we selectively filter the facts and focus on evidence that supports our behaviors. It's been shown that our brains validate the "rightness" of our decisions by ignoring evidence that might prove contrary. Psychologists call this *cognitive dissonance*. And it has profound implications for how we make decisions. Unless we are aware of this phenomenon, and unless we deliberately ask others whom we trust to give us their independent view, we have no idea whether or not we are seeing a situation objectively.

The body of evidence is surprisingly large. And it shows that the people who consider themselves the most competent are actually the least competent. (Score one for the importance of staying humble!) For example, in research published in 2000,[4] researchers showed that people who score lowest on a series of simple tests of reading and spelling actually believed themselves to be the most proficient. In contrast, researchers found competent people were more likely to underestimate their performance. In other words, there is a reverse correlation between how we evaluate our performance—and how we actually perform.

This research echoes other studies showing that overconfidence is rampant. For example, researchers have shown that the vast majority of people rate themselves "above average" in a wide variety of activities, despite the statistical impossibility of that conclusion. It's like Garrison Keillor's Lake Wobegon come to life, where the women are handsome and all the men are "above average."

Here's a further twist to this body of research. The tests showed that the people who were revealed in earlier tests to be more incompetent were unaffected by the experience of seeing how well other people performed. Some people in this group even further inflated their estimates of their abilities, based purely on seeing other people's scores. In other words, if you're not very competent, it's very difficult to dissuade you from your position. You are one obstinate fellow!

Why did this come about? The "assumption of competence" is thought to have conferred an evolutionary advantage tens of thousands of years ago—when our ancestors were hunting large animals (think woolly mammoths). They had no weapons—only sharp sticks. The only way for these early hunters to succeed was to band together. The assumption of competence provided them with the collective courage to do something that no individual in his right mind would choose to do on his own. Minus the assumption of competence, they would have sensibly stayed in their caves. The assumption of competence helped them overcome their fears, take on big challenges, feel successful, and propagate the species (even if a few of them died each time a mammoth was killed).

The assumption of competence causes us to justify our beliefs and decisions—even if they're boneheaded or downright dangerous—and then surround ourselves with like-minded folks. In the words of Franz Kafka, "a belief is like a guillotine—just as heavy and just as light." The assumption of competence explains why people develop hardened political and religious positions. It's the deep ghost in the machine. No wonder the word "assume" can also be read as: "the ass you made of me."

We can't escape the assumption of competence, but we can minimize it when we are managing decisions. Here's where consultative decision making really shines. If we are on guard against the assumption of competence, and aware of our fallibility, we can see the importance of surrounding ourselves with smart people with different points of view who can help us appreciate what's really going on. The consultative process is invaluable because it helps us view the problem more objectively—and see the flaws in our own machine more clearly.

THE DANGER OF "WORKAROUNDS"

Decisions can be very difficult to manage in settings where people aren't used to accepting responsibility—or where the structure works against it. Position accountability (what the position is accountable for) and responsibility (what the person actually can do) can get wildly out of synch. This often is due to what we call "nichifying."

For botanists, biologists, and other scientists, the idea of nichifying is central to understanding how evolution works. Plants and animals are in a constant struggle to find and occupy the safest and easiest niche for their survival. As the climate changes, for example, plants move to wetter or drier ground. As predators become more prevalent, animals move to less dangerous territory.

Within organizations, people nichify as well. When it's positive, people seek niches where their talent is most valued, where they feel most productive, where they feel they can best contribute. In these cases, nichifying works to the organization's advantage.

But nichifying has a negative side. It shows up in bureaucracies in the form of "workarounds"—instances where people do the work someone else is responsible for, typically because they do it better or enjoy it more. People will say: "Well, if you really want to get that done, you have to see Dorothy in Accounting. Even though she's not in charge of Procurement, everything passes through her."

Public agencies are prone to nichifying because civil service rules prevent people from moving easily to find their best niche. Work responsibilities flow toward people with the skills to do the work, not necessarily the people in the appropriate roles. Workarounds result in "shadow organizations"—an informal organization on top of the formal one you see on paper. Where shadow organizations have been allowed to flourish, the result is confusion about roles and responsibilities as well as convoluted decision making.

For example, financial decisions at one California state agency were divided among three departments. Accounts receivable and payable were under the Finance Department. The Operations Department handled capital expenditures. And the Department of Planning dealt with budgets, planning, and sophisticated financing. People within the organization understood who did what—but no one was accountable for financial performance. No surprise, then, that this agency had very poor financial performance overall.

What can you do to manage decisions well in such a setting? For one thing, you can spend extra time with people, building trust and support for changing the work processes. You can call attention to the gap between the "paper" organization and the actual one. You can fight to put people where their talents can best be aligned with their real job responsibilities. You can also continually look for opportunities to recruit and promote talented people in the organization. Otherwise, the talented people are likely to leave—triggering further bureaucracy.

• • •

CONCLUSION

To build trust, you need to focus on becoming a superb decision *manager*. This means teaching people the vocabulary of decision making; it means designing effective decision processes; it means avoiding the trap of faux consensus. Above all, it means being clear about delegations.

Effective leaders help people see the implications of the "assumption of competence." They train themselves and others to question their assumptions and to keep an open mind. In so doing, they model the kind of open and collaborative communication that is so important to developing a high-performing organization. When faced with a tough "right vs. right" decision, effective leaders see themselves as stewards. They look to the core values, consult deeply, reach a moment of resolve, communicate the decision, and move on. We should do the same—and move on to learning about how your personal qualities as a leader can help inspire trust.

PRACTICE #5

START WITH YOURSELF

(ACV+STF+LTO+MDW+SWY) + (APC+SCF+SST+MTC+APQ) = LC

When Franklin Roosevelt was running for president in 1932, a reporter asked him what he thought the job entailed. "The presidency is not merely an administrative office," he replied. "It is preeminently a place of moral leadership. All our great presidents were leaders of thought in times when certain historic ideas in the life of the nation had to be clarified."

Roosevelt provided thought leadership to the nation. But he also provided something else: he displayed four personal qualities that are necessary to build trust. In this chapter, I'm going to focus on those personal qualities. Like professional practices, these personal qualities can be *learned*. They may not be easy. But they are within everyone's reach. Warren Bennis has said, "The most dangerous leadership myth is that leaders are born. In fact, the opposite is true. Leaders are made rather than born."[1]

HONOR

On December 11, 1995, Aaron Feuerstein was celebrating his seventieth birthday in a Boston restaurant. Life was good. His company, Malden Mills, had just finished building a new Polartec factory in Lawrence, Massachusetts—the first mill to be built in New England in over one hundred years. Then, in the middle of dinner, he received a phone call informing him that his mill was on fire. "It's a six-alarm blaze," he was told. "Some people are hurt."

Feuerstein rushed to the scene. Shortly afterward, a shaken Feuerstein spoke to his employees gathered in a high school gym. They steeled themselves to hear the bad news. Thirty-three workers were injured—eight critically. Three buildings had been destroyed.

PRACTICE #5: START WITH YOURSELF

....

Leaders need to display four personal qualities to build high levels of trust among the people around them. They need to be honorable, show enthusiasm and passion for what they do, display a well-rounded sense of humor, and stay humble and curious. In addition, they need to become master communicators and be adept at dealing with the complex, and sometimes paradoxical, personal issues that leaders face. When blended together, these are the qualities that build trust.

Most of the workers assumed that Feuerstein would take the $300 million in insurance money and relocate. After all, most manufacturers from New England had already moved production to cheaper, nonunion places in the Sunbelt or overseas. Instead, Feuerstein promised to rebuild the mill. He also promised to pay all three thousand of his workers their December wage as well as a Christmas bonus. He kept all the employees on the payroll with full benefits for three months. He didn't consider this charity, but rather saw it as good business sense and in keeping with his views on social responsibility. In one week, his promises cost him $1.5 million in payroll. His employees called him a hero. His honorable behavior earned him their undying loyalty.[2]

Honorable leaders live up to their commitments. They make no promise that they can't keep. Their word is their bond. They follow a code of reciprocity that enables other people to trust them—and to want to follow them. In the words of Rushworth Kidder, founder of the Institute of Global Ethics, it's "adherence to the unenforceable."[3] Taking responsibility, giving credit where credit is due, behaving morally and ethically— these are the habits of the honorable person.

THE 4 Hs OF LEADERSHIP

HONOR	HEART
Follows a moral and ethical code that enables others to place a high level of trust in them.	Has a passion for what they do. Wants to press on in the face of disappointment and loss.
HUMILITY	HUMOR
Channels ego needs toward the larger goal of building a great culture.	Maintains a sense of humor about themselves and what life has brought them.

Living honorably means thinking through what is right and then acting on it. It means doing the honorable thing—even when the stakes are high and doing the right thing carries great risk. Living honorably is about upholding an ethical code that spans all religions and faiths.

One of my favorite quotes is from Mark Twain. "Always do right," he penned. "This will gratify some people, and astonish the rest."

HEART

As a young man in his twenties, Walt Disney drove himself night and day to realize his dream of creating the first full-length animated cartoon. He nearly bankrupted his young company in the process. But after seven years of struggle, he completed his masterpiece, *Snow White and the Seven Dwarfs*, and it made cinematic history.

Later, as a man in his forties, Walt once again drove his organization to the brink of disaster in order to realize his dream of Disneyland. Was he a reckless risk taker? No, Walt Disney simply had an incredible passion for what he believed in—and he had the courage and heart to see it through.

Leading from the heart cannot be feigned or coached. Leading from the heart means suffering grave disappointments and experiencing the metaphoric deaths that all leaders must go through. What distinguishes successful leaders is their ability to sustain their passion through adversity.

As author Lance Secretan[4] puts it: "Leadership is not a formula or a program, it is a human activity that comes from the heart."

In the corporate world, there are dozens of examples of successful leaders who lead from their hearts. Kirk Perron, the founder of Jamba Juice, established his first juice store in San Luis Obispo in the 1990s. From the start, he had a vision to inspire and simplify healthy living.[5] Richard Branson, the founder of Virgin Records and Virgin Airways, espouses the importance of following one's passions. "To me, business isn't about wearing suits or pleasing stockholders. It's about being true to yourself, your ideas and focusing on the essentials."[6] Through Apple's meteoric rise in the 1980s and its rebirth after his return in the late 1990s, Steve Jobs had a passion for blending art and computing. "I've always said that Apple is the most creatively advanced technical company," he said.[7]

In short, effective leaders are sustained by an inner energy and drive. They are passionate about what they do and that passion inspires the people around them and builds trust—as well as spark.

HUMILITY

What's the most important attribute people look for in their managers and leaders? A study of most admired CEOs cited humility as the number-one factor—their willingness to accept and admit their flaws.[8]

Humble leaders aren't focused on themselves. They use the word "we" twice as much as the word "me." What is it that makes humility such an attractive quality? It all goes back to trust and reciprocity. We assume a humble person is more likely to do what's in the best interest of ourselves and of the group. So when someone acts in a humble manner, our cheater meter swings toward "trust."

Alan Brunacini was fire chief for the city of Phoenix for more than thirty years. He created a culture that values humility. Brunacini lists specific traits he expects of his employees. Among them:

- Talk less, listen more.
- Build trust in yourself by trusting others.
- Become more emotionally literate.
- Stop micromanaging.

- Lighten up and let go.
- Laugh more.
- Don't hurt people's feelings (understand people's feelings).

Effective leaders like Chief Brunacini check their egos at the door. They channel their ego needs toward the larger goal of building a great organization. This aspect of leadership—taking your ego out of it—is the key to building trust. If your underlying orientation is to put yourself first, your communication will betray your "me-ness." On the other hand, if your underlying orientation is toward treating other people as equals, people will perceive you as someone who is fair, who can be trusted.

I've known managers and leaders who've undergone shifts in their internal orientation. One talked of having his wife leave him, going through psychotherapy, and then winning her back. Another talked of helping his daughter go through treatment for self-abusive behavior. He said her recovery made him more committed to his own personal growth. Yet another talked of watching an egotistical boss lay waste to his company—and vowing to never repeat the mistake.

I remember well the CEO of a public utility company who always deflected praise and recognition away from herself—and onto her employees. When her board of directors presented her an award for outstanding service, she turned to the employees gathered behind her and presented the award to them. "I don't deserve this. It's our employees who deserve it," she said.

People can learn humility at any age. One mid-level retail store manager, branded "arrogant" by his peers, went through a course of coaching and self-reflection and found what he called the key: "The very fact of expressing my humility made me feel more powerful. There's nothing better than letting go of the feeling you have to be perfect."

An executive for a Cleveland-based steel company said: "I remember living through a firefight in Vietnam thinking I was going to die. I've never felt more grateful than when the chopper picked us up. Being alive is all I ask for." That executive has been credited with building a company in which trust permeates everything, from its "no questions" guarantee of its products to the company's website, which features personal profiles of all 2,200 employees.

WHAT WENT WRONG AT ENRON?

....

If you talk to people who worked at Enron before its fall in 2003, many good things were happening. Talented people were being hired and empowered to make decisions. Creative deals were being struck. An extraordinary business model was emerging for trading in energy futures and managing risk on a global scale. Enron's amazing rise was a case study being taught at leading business schools. So what went wrong?

The failure of Enron was, at its core, a failure of personal leadership. Chairman Kenneth Lay was ambitious yet inattentive to the workings of the huge behemoth he created. CEO Jeff Skilling was an arrogant risk taker, willing to bend the legal limits. Andrew Fastow was a financial whiz kid intent on siphoning off millions for his personal use. These leaders of Enron built a fortune by transforming the marketplace for natural gas and then for other commodities. But in their quest for profits, Lay, Skilling, Fastow, and company flouted fundamental moral and ethical values. Ironically, the downfall would not have occurred had they adhered to Enron's own code of ethics:

Respect: We treat others as we would like to be treated ourselves. We do not tolerate abusive or disrespectful treatment. Ruthlessness, callousness, and arrogance don't belong here.

Integrity: We work with customers and prospects openly, honestly, and sincerely. When we say we will do something, we do it; when we say we cannot or will not do something, then we don't do it.

Communication: We have an obligation to communicate. Here, we take the time to talk with one another and to listen. We believe that information is meant to move and that information moves people.

Excellence: We are satisfied with nothing less than the very best in everything we do. We will continue to raise the bar for everyone. The great fun here will be for all of us to discover just how good we can really be.[9]

These values mirror the personal qualities discussed in this chapter. But in Enron's case, those values were only on paper.

HUMOR

Herb Kelleher's antics were legendary at Southwest. He dressed up like Elvis for Halloween. He once arm-wrestled a competitor's CEO over a trademark dispute. "We've always believed that business can and should be fun," he says. "At far too many companies, when you come into the office, you put on a mask. You look different, talk different, and act different—which is why most business encounters are, at best, bland and impersonal."

It is for this reason that Southwest uses the "humor test." Applicants are asked: "Tell us how humor helped you get around one of the more difficult situations in your life." Prospective pilots are asked to don khaki shorts and Hawaiian shirts. Those who have fun with it pass the test. Those who resist flunk. They don't have the right stuff for Southwest.

Almost every successful leader I've worked with uses self-deprecating humor. Dee Hock, the founder of Visa, describes the good fortune that put him in the right place at the right time to create the world's largest credit card company. "Pure accident is all it was," he says. "I was foolish enough to volunteer." Jim Rouse, founder and CEO of the Rouse Company, would tell his employees: "I'm not sure I perform any meaningful function here. So thank you for letting me serve as your CEO."

John F. Kennedy said he didn't know where Jackie kept all his money.

When 1984 Democratic presidential nominee Walter Mondale accused Ronald Reagan of "government by amnesia," the president countered with, "I thought that remark accusing me of having amnesia was uncalled for. I just wish I could remember who said it."

People love leaders who display a sense of humor. When you poke fun at yourself, our cheater meters swing toward "trust." If love is the universal language, then humor is the universal trust builder.

BECOMING A MASTER COMMUNICATOR

The word communication literally means "to make common." At its most basic level, it means letting your needs be known. At its highest level, communication means building strong, trusting relationships with people whose perspectives are very different from your own. The educator and psychotherapist Virginia Satir wrote, "Once a human being has arrived on this earth, communication is the largest single factor determining what kinds of relationships he makes with others and what happens to him in the world."[10]

Much of my work in developing leaders and leading organizations focuses on communication. Since publishing *Straight Talk* in 1998,[11] I've continued to develop my understanding that people can develop four different levels—or "powers"—of communication.

THE FOUR POWERS OF COMMUNICATION

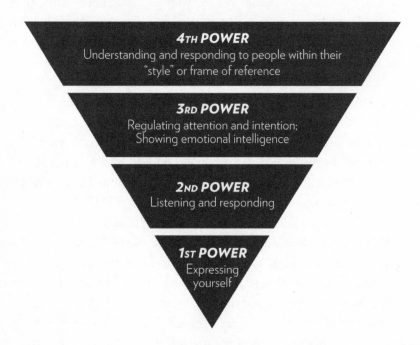

4TH POWER
Understanding and responding to people within their "style" or frame of reference

3RD POWER
Regulating attention and intention;
Showing emotional intelligence

2ND POWER
Listening and responding

1ST POWER
Expressing
yourself

The First Power: Expressing Yourself. From the moment we pop out of the womb, we start expressing what we want. Over time, we learn how to use words. We learn how to name simple emotional and mental states. By the time we're adults, we've developed a full array of strategies to express how we feel and what we want.

Yet even as adults, we are still working on this first power. Adults, rather than getting straight to the heart of what they want, often beat around the bush, deflecting attention from the real issue or need out of the fear of losing "face"—a fear of exposure, a fear they will look silly, a fear they will lose authority or power. Yet learning how to express ourselves even when it feels emotionally charged and sensitive is all part of mastering the first power.

The Second Power: Listening and Responding. Soon after we pop out of the womb, we also begin learning how to respond to others. We laugh at funny faces. We sense other people's moods. As we gain the use of language, we respond with words. By the time most of us reach age five or six, we can share our thoughts and feelings with another person and build fledgling relationships.

As we grow older, we learn how to participate in a conversation, recognizing that the other person deserves our respect and attention. We begin to establish patterns of speaking and listening based on the notion of reciprocity and trust building.

At a more advanced level, people who master this second power can extract a deeper meaning from a conversation than simply what is said. They can paraphrase what they've heard. They can interpret what someone means and add layers of meaning to it.

They can validate their interpretation and, by so doing, create deeper bonds of trust with other people.

The Third Power: Regulating Attention and Intention. People with the third power show a level of self-awareness and self-control that distinguishes them from second-power communicators. People with this power can vary their level of attention and their level of intent, thereby achieving high levels of emotional intelligence. Let's talk about attention first. There are four levels:

- **Level 1:** Volition. Am I actively paying attention? Or is my attention wandering?
- **Level 2:** Consciousness. Am I in a highly conscious state or a routine state?
- **Level 3:** Affinity. Am I attracted to or repelled by the communication?
- **Level 4:** Quality. Is my attention creative, analytical, or empathetic? Am I varying it based on the situation?[11]

Third-power communicators are aware of the quality of their attention and display the social and political awareness to select the appropriate setting. For example, if they're listening to someone who's having problems with a colleague, they may choose to respond analytically: "I've had similar experiences. I know what you're going through. Here's how I handled it." Or empathetically: "I can really appreciate how you feel. How can I help?" Or creatively: "It's amazing that happened to you. Let's think of some ways you could deal with the situation."

Third-power communicators are also conscious of their intent and can vary it. There are four types of intent: affirmative, controlling, defensive, and relinquishing. Only the first is positive. The others lead to conflict. Third-power communicators are able to use an affirming intent 90 percent of the time. Even in the middle of a heated debate, they'll say: "I hear what you're saying and I respect your views—even though we disagree."

Regulating the levels of attention and intent enables third-power communicators to show a high level of emotional intelligence. Daniel Goleman, who popularized the term "emotional intelligence," has shown that the most successful leaders display emotional intelligence competencies like self-awareness, self-regulation, motivation, empathy, and social skill and are therefore able to build deeper and more satisfying relationships.[12]

Part of emotional intelligence is speaking consciously from the "I." For example, rather than saying "that wasn't clear" to someone who just suggested an idea, you could say: "I feel confused. Can you clarify this for me?" People with this power can also communicate subtle nuances and flavors of emotions. For example, you might say to a colleague who's just gotten promoted: "I'm jealous you got that promotion, but I'm also really happy for you. Excuse me if I seem just a bit conflicted."

In sum, to assess your third-power skills, ask yourself: "Am I conscious of my attention? Do I exert control over it? When I'm listening, am I fully in the conversation? Do I tune my mind to hear not only the things the other person is saying, but the things she is *not* saying? Do I ask good, affirming questions designed to deepen my understanding? Do I affirm the other person's point of view, even if I disagree with it?"

If you can answer yes to these questions most of the time, then it's a good sign you've mastered the third power of communication.

The Fourth Power: Understanding People's Styles. People with the fourth power can take their communication one step further: they can vary their communication *based on an accurate understanding of the other person's communication style and the assumptions that underlie that style.* They have the self-awareness to identify the other person's frame of reference and adapt their own style accordingly—and thus help facilitate productive communication among people with different and often conflicting points of view.

To master the fourth power, you have to recognize that even when people are speaking the same language, they may be talking and listening *past each other* within different frames of reference and operating assumptions. You have to learn how to identify these different styles, and then learn how to vary your communication style depending on the situation. The fourth power means knowing how to foster better communication by varying your style.

In my book *Straight Talk*, I described the four different communication styles: the Director, Expresser, Thinker, and Harmonizer. Each of these styles, which I described in the previous chapter, operates from a different set of assumptions.[13] People are not simply one of these styles, but an amalgam of all four. To understand your style, you need to know how strongly you exhibit each of them.

The fourth power encompasses the highest level of self-awareness. People with this power can use their understanding of different styles to shape how they listen. This is truly powerful listening. As they listen, they can quickly identify the underlying frame of reference and respond in that frame. For the person being listened to, it's an amazing experience. "I feel truly understood by her when I'm talking with her," is how one person describes it.

A former dean at Harvard Business School is a fourth-power communicator. When talking to a Thinker, she could be very detailed and analytical. When talking to an Expresser, she would animatedly tell stories and joke around. When talking to a Director, she would cut right to the chase, and the discussion would be over in five minutes. And when talking to a Harmonizer, she would begin with some small talk before introducing the real topic of discussion.

What's important about the fourth power is that it can be learned. You can learn your own style (at www.straight-talk-now.com). You then need to learn how to decipher other people's styles.

FIVE UNEXPECTED QUALITIES OF LEADERS

"I don't know anyone who planned to be here," a CEO of a software company remarked during a forum for CEOs. "I think I got here because of a combination of luck, character, and divine design."

It's true that you can't plot your course exactly. But here are five unexpected qualities of virtually every great leader I've worked with.

Go to grow. If you look at their resumes, successful leaders tend to move around a lot, especially early in their careers. Every three or four years, they move on to another challenge, often moving from one organization to another, and then back again to the first. "They go to grow," as one person put it. This growth gives them a wealth of perspective that enables them to manage effectively, no matter what the situation.

Leaders are readers. If you look at their bedside tables, leaders tend to read voraciously. Reading teaches people to process information at multiple levels and dimensions quickly. This helps them bring clarity and sensitivity to a situation. "He thinks in a way that allows me to clear away the underbrush and see the forest," is how one executive describes his boss.

Hire and fire. Effective leaders know how to take care of other people—but not at the expense of their company. They demonstrate at an early point in their careers that they can handle the responsibility of firing people. As one put it: "I seem blessed with the ability to fire people without them resenting it."

Tolerance. Effective leaders show a high level of tolerance for different political views, religious beliefs, and worldviews. Typically, they've been around enough to understand why people adopt different views, and don't take it personally when their view differs from someone else's. As the CEO of a software company put it, "A good leader knows when to engage in a healthy debate, and when debate is futile." If the issue relates to personal beliefs or cultural values, effective leaders show respect and appreciation, and build trust among people from all sorts of different and diverse backgrounds.

The Network. In comparison to others, effective leaders tend to build large networks of people to whom they can turn for business advice, personal counsel, or simply to learn what's going on in other parts of the world. And it doesn't hurt that this network provides a large number of opportunities for jobs, should the leader decide to "go to grow" again.

FOUR PARADOXES OF LEADERSHIP

It is only the great thinker who is exposed to what I call paradoxes, which are nothing else than grand thoughts in embryo.

—Søren Kierkegaard

Change is difficult enough. But for people in leadership roles, change can be made even more difficult because the way forward is never clear. Everywhere you look there are difficult, sometimes paradoxical, situations. Here are four examples that you may have to grapple with. How you grapple with them will help define your success as a leader.

The Ambition Balance: True leaders are ambitious—but their ambitions are in service to something greater than themselves. Peter Drucker, the famed management consultant, describes it as a singular focus on defining what the organization needs. When Louis Gerstner took over at IBM, he saw the need for far greater customer focus. When Jack Welch took over at General Electric, he saw the need to divest the company of any business that wasn't number one or two in its marketplace. When Darwin Smith took over at Kimberly-Clark, he saw the need to sell the mills and focus on the paper products business. Make no mistake: each of these men was ambitious. But more important, all believed they knew what it was that the organization needed from them. No one told Gerstner or Welch or Smith to do these things. Each had the ambition to get it done. At the same time, these were the things that *needed* to be done.

The Assumption Trap: Leaders need to make tough decisions—and yet almost always those decisions are based on a set of assumptions. One of the most pervasive assumptions in our society is that we are powerful actors, capable of solving any problem if we just tackle it rationally. We assume we can affect major outcomes through the force of our will. We assume our competence, act on the basis of that assumption, and then we defend our assumption to the hilt. Even when confronted with contrary evidence, we continue to defend our assumptions out of a fear not to be exposed as silly or foolish. Fear is the mind killer. And assumptions are the accomplice, driving the getaway car.

The path through the assumption paradox is recognizing the underlying fear at work—the fear of self-exposure—and finding the courage to discuss your assumptions and admit your mistakes to others. This means that *you, the leader*, are the first to admit your mistakes. No one can be right if everyone is wrong, goes the old axiom. But, on the other hand, no one can be right if everyone's right. You have to set the tone for others.

Differing Worldviews: To be a leader in an era of increasing globalization and diversity, you need to open yourself to understanding different worldviews. Our Western worldview schools us to look at everything rationally. This worldview is not comfortable with uncertainty and irrationality. Perhaps that's why Westerners enjoy neat plot lines that play so well on television. It's comforting to see sixty-minute solutions, easy outs, and resolvable dilemmas. When faced with a problem, our first instinct is to take it apart and devise the best solution. Assuming the world is inherently ordered and rational, that's not a bad strategy. Unfortunately, this worldview does not prepare us for dynamic complexity, or chaos, or for seeing the world through the lens of other worldviews.

Philosophers and sociologists have identified at least three other worldviews: the Eastern, the Existentialist, and the Religious.

The Eastern worldview focuses on what is unknowable. It holds that intuition and insight can help us tap into deeper areas of spiritual meaning. It assumes that the unconscious mind has access to deeper and more meaningful insights than those available through rational thinking, and that this nonconscious awareness can be improved through training. In the Eastern worldview, people act under the influence of unseen spiritual forces, and their lives are suffused with this unseen spiritual world. People with this worldview have a deep psychological need for meditation, for quieting the rational mind, for a personal experience of the unknowable. They also distrust easy solutions to complex problems.

A third worldview is the Existentialist, which holds that life, as it is experienced by human beings, is fundamentally unexplainable, but that we owe it to ourselves to make the best of the hand we're dealt, both in terms of our family and the world into which we are born. This worldview holds that the highest goal is to be authentic to one's own beliefs, to act on those beliefs, and to create a life built on being true to those beliefs. Existentialist thinkers such as Søren Kierkegaard or Jean-Paul Sartre view human beings as forced to deal with circumstances way outside their control—and having no choice but to find meaning by discovering what's truly important to each individual. A corollary to this worldview is that what's important to you has no bearing on what's important to me. We must each discover our individual truth in our own way.

The fourth worldview, the Religious, holds that knowledge is conferred through faith, and that a kind of mystical power is vested in God or a system of gods. People operating under this paradigm have a deep psychological need for prayer and religious experience—and they base their decisions on beliefs and traditions rooted in religion. This worldview confers great power on religious leaders who interpret events in the external world as the manifestation of God's intent and try to impose their interpretations through religious training and teaching.

All four of these worldviews mingle together in today's organizations. To be an effective leader, you need to gently navigate the contradictions between these worldviews. A well-developed sense of humor helps. But it's also important to establish a culture in which people with different worldviews share a common set of core values (see Chapter 1). How effectively you build trust among people with these different worldviews will be a test of your leadership.

The Succession Paradox: It has often been said that the true test of a leader is how well he plans for his departure. The question isn't whether you have a succession plan. It's how capable you are in surrounding yourself with people truly capable of taking your place and running the show. And therein lies the paradox.

Some of the seemingly most successful leaders fail to find the path through this paradox. They can't handle the challenge of surrounding themselves with people who are able to do their jobs. Again and again, we see examples of leaders failing to deal with the succession paradox.

On the other hand, we also see great success stories. At one of our client companies, the CEO surrounded herself with a senior staff of highly capable leaders. Her board of directors knew that should something happen to her, there was a surfeit of worthy successors. At another, the CEO of a construction company changed the management structure to give three able colleagues the opportunity to buy into the firm.

Cutting through the succession paradox is easy once you let go of the notion of your own indispensability. It's another fear you have to overcome—a fear of the unknown. For some this is hard to do, but it's a necessary step in building trust.

· · ·

CONCLUSION

To lead successfully, you need to have certain personal qualities—heart, honor, humility, and humor. I call these the 4 Hs. You also need to learn how to be a master communicator, effectively using all four powers to control your intention and your attention, show emotional intelligence, and respond to people from within their own frame of reference or "style."

This chapter also discussed why effective leaders need to be comfortable with paradox: leaders are chosen based on the congruence between the behaviors they manifest and the values that pertain in their *culture*. But what does this mean in a global organization? Ideas and notions about leadership can vary dramatically depending on where you are located— from country to country, office to office—even within the same building. Effective leaders know that while the organization operates in many cultures and worldviews, the organization has its own set of core values. They make a priority of ensuring that the core values of that culture are understood by every employee and customer.

When you put all these qualities together, you get one word: "integrity." The word literally means "to be whole, unimpaired." It conveys the notion of being trustworthy. It also implies the ability to think and act in ways that may be counter to the prevailing winds, but in ways that flow out of, in Roosevelt's words, "a place of moral leadership."

ACCELERATE THE PACE OF CHANGE

(ACV+STF+LTO+MDW+SWY) + (APC+SCF+SST+MTC+APQ) = LC

Don Winkler, the former chairman of Finance One Corporation, was once assigned the task of managing the subsidiary of an American bank in Greece. When he arrived in Athens, he discovered the bank was in deep trouble. Scores of customers were closing their accounts, appalled by the poor quality of customer service.

Winkler knew he had to change the bank's culture. He also knew that in order to be successful he needed to get the bank's Greek executives and employees fully engaged and committed to making the change happen.

He convened several brainstorming sessions. Initially, he encountered resistance, especially among the Greek managers of the bank who resented Don's outside intrusion. But Winkler kept at it.

After the tenth brainstorming session, the executive team came up with a plan. The Greek bank president decided he would move his desk into the middle of the lobby. This would symbolize the bank's new commitment to customer service.

An advertising campaign kicked off the event. Customers came to see the bank president sitting at his desk as they came through the doors. But as Winkler recounts it, something surprising happened. The Greek president heard customers complain firsthand. The level of vitriol directed at the bank shocked him. "We must do something," he told his executive team. "Immediately."

The bank president ordered a new customer complaint tracking system. He insisted that all employees be trained to respond immediately to customer concerns. The bank president personally presided over the customer service team. As the level of customer service went up, the bank's business was revitalized. In less than six months, the bank's customers were singing the bank's praises. In less than five years, the bank realized a 5,000 percent increase in profits.[1]

There are two takeaways from Winkler's story. One is that you have to get close to your customers to know what is really going on. Second, employees need to be engaged in an accelerated learning process. Winkler's ideas worked because he understood that employees could be agents of change only if they were given the knowledge and the means to invent the change themselves. As Winkler says, "They alone could identify the continuing sequence of small changes that add value, enhance efficiency, build competitive leadership, and increase profits." They alone could accelerate the learning.

PRACTICE #6:
ACCELERATE THE PACE OF CHANGE

....

In a time of accelerating change, people need to learn quickly and adapt quickly. It's the leader's job to put the necessary systems in place to do that, just as Winkler did. I call these systems "learning loops." Successful learning loops have three qualities: they are based on clear metrics and targets; people empowered to make change monitor them on a regular basis; and the communication is immediate.

Effective leaders arm people with the skills and tools to continuously learn, adapt, and navigate change by putting learning loops into place throughout the organization. They also weed out hidden "ignorance loops" that impede the organization from learning.

WHY ACCELERATE THE PACE OF CHANGE

Every leader of a company today lives in fear of the disruptive innovation: the new technology, new service, or new government policy that enables customers to bypass your industry completely and get the same service or product from another source. It happened in the newspaper business, when online services stripped away its near monopoly on classified advertising. It happened in the telephony industry, when cell phones decimated the business model of the "Baby Bells." It happened in the banking business when deregulation enabled retail banks to move into investment banking. It's happening in the energy industry today.

To spark the kind of innovation that enables companies to change and adapt and not be displaced, you need to accelerate the pace of change and arm people with the ability to think—and act—strategically. The newspaper industry knew the change was coming. It just couldn't see the extent of it or plan well for it, because it couldn't see the full benefit of cannibalizing its existing business to enter into a new business. As the CEO of one newspaper group put it, "We didn't appreciate the scale of change."

The best way to lead in a time of accelerating change is to keep the foot on the accelerator. Which accelerator? I call it the "learning accelerator." When learning happens, change occurs. If you install the right systems of communication and learning, you will experience higher levels of information sharing, trust, innovation, and performance.

LEARNING LOOPS

Bill Weiss, former CEO of Ameritech, describes his experience leading people through change as follows: "It's a race where you run the first four laps as fast as you can—and then you gradually increase the speed."

To accelerate the pace of change, leaders must focus on creating systems of learning. It sounds easy, but it's not. The secret is what I call "learning loops." Learning loops are similar to feedback loops except they are deliberately designed to achieve organizational change at maximum speed. Toyota and Honda pioneered the practice of learning loops in the 1950s and 1960s when they organized people into teams and gave those teams the power to measure their performance and improve. The "virtuous" circle of learning, innovation, and higher performance—what the Japanese call *kaizen*—has since been put to use in many manufacturing sectors. Our firm has worked with a wide array of clients to implement learning loops—and we've yet to find an industry, or a business process, that doesn't improve when we do so.

Learning loops have three critical elements:

- **They have things to measure (metrics and targets).** How are you measuring customer satisfaction? How about service reliability? Or safety or environmental protection? If you've read Chapter 1, then you know these metrics should be tied to your core values. Your metrics need to be figured out and translated into an ongoing system and process of measurement. Things can't be measured once and forgotten. You need a continuous cycle of measurement to understand the trend over time.

- **Real-time or near real-time communication about the metrics needs to occur with people who are empowered to make change happen.** The right forums need to be put in place and visibly supported by management. People need to be encouraged to take the time to talk about the data and figure out ways to improve the company's performance. They also need to trust that the learning loops are intended to create change, not trigger reprisals. The executive of a bank purposefully invokes a "no reprisals" rule at the start of every learning loop meeting. He says: "There can be no reprisals for anything said in this room, so long as it is stated with the interest of the company at heart."

- **Real change needs to occur as a result of the learning loops.** It's not enough to generate ideas. Senior management must support and implement innovations that flower from the learning loop forums. Those innovations need to be tracked to determine whether they are successful and, if so, implemented across the organization.

As people begin to trust that the intent is not to penalize but to learn and adapt, they start to experience the power of learning loops and see real improvement. Often it begins with comparison of performance across teams. One of our clients, a revenue collections agency, deploys teams of tax collectors and auditors in district offices across the state. As we worked with them to install learning loops, they began to measure things like the timeliness of tax filings, the efficiency of collections, and the effectiveness of tax audits. Over time, the teams started to talk about which districts were more effective in each aspect of the business. Some districts were more effective at tax audits, for example. It turns out they were using a specific modeling tool for predicting which audits would yield the most revenue. As a result, other districts adopted the same model and experienced real improvement.

LEARNING LOOP

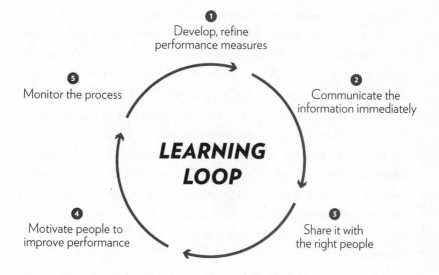

THE ROLE OF CONVERSATION

Change happens because people talk. Conversation is the work that people must do to change. The problem is, most leaders forget that their role is to create forums where people can talk about their work, ask what could be improved, and listen to their suggestions. Without this conversation, change is not possible.

THE IMPORTANCE OF TALK

....

People often ask me what the secret is to high-performing organizations. I surprise them by saying: "Talk." As consultants, one of the first things we look for is the level of talk, the quality of talk, and who's doing the talking. Here's a typical example. At a large California nonprofit, we discovered that the leadership team, consisting of the CEO, COO, and two senior program leaders, met weekly. At the next level, a group of ten mid-level managers met weekly as well. But despite these meetings, actions across departments were not well coordinated. Goals weren't being met. There was a lack of accountability and performance. As we dug deeper, we found that one mid-level manager had been named the "liaison" to the leadership team. Her job was to carry problems to the leaders and to ferry back solutions.

We facilitated a meeting with the leadership team and asked them how this system was working. "Frankly, it's hard to tell," said the COO. "We wanted them to have a forum of their own so they could gel as a team." Remarked the CEO: "Maybe so, but things aren't getting done. And that's a problem."

We suggested that the "liaison" role was blurring lines of accountability. We suggested they consider eliminating the mid-managers' meeting, substituting for it a biweekly meeting between senior leadership and mid-level managers. In these meetings, either the CEO or the COO should always be present—and the focus should be on results, finding out where problems were occurring, and asking why. "Talk about your business plan, what results you're getting, and what's needed to improve results," we said. "Talk only about that."

The CEO embraced the idea and it was implemented the next month. It quickly surfaced that the mid-level managers were fretting over staff allocations. Resources were not being shared. The liaison said she was glad to no longer be caught in the middle. The CEO began asking tough questions. The managers began focusing on performance rather than head count. One particularly territorial manager was moved aside. Over the next six months, the others showed significant gains.

We see the same pattern all the time. While the specifics may differ, in organizations where talk (the right talk among the right people) is emphasized, trust, accountability, performance, and success are also present.

What are some of the characteristics of these forums? First, they are honest. There's no penalty for speaking your mind or challenging the status quo. Second, the discussion is data driven. While people are free to speak their minds, they are challenged to explain their reasoning and the data that supports their conclusions. Third, it's grounded in the idea that the conversation shouldn't be about the work. The conversation *is* the work. From talking comes real change.

This failure to engage people in real, honest conversation saps the creative energy of organizations. It leaves people feeling frustrated. Managers pull out their hair, wondering why trust is low and innovation nonexistent. The answer is simple: the organization's leaders have failed to create the type of engagement that inspires people to learn and pour their best selves into their work.

A certain type of manager squelches conversation almost by instinct. They operate out of a need to dominate and direct. They try to coerce behavior. They'll tell people they want to see a 5 percent increase in quality, or a 10 percent increase in output, without creating forums in which people can talk about how well the system itself is working, identify problems, and suggest solutions. These kinds of managers nearly always come up short—and their organizations with them.

Honest, open engagement is crucial to building a high-performing organization. A good leader understands this and creates conversational forums that embolden people to change.

PROBLEMS WITH LEARNING LOOPS

By their very nature, learning loops involve people at the front lines of the company, since they are the ones who ultimately effectuate change. So long as those people trust management, the introduction of learning loops should be relatively easy. But when people at the front lines distrust management, then it can be extraordinarily tough to install learning loops. People will suspect that the learning loops are not designed for learning, but instead as a way to weed out underperforming teams and individuals. They will stand shoulder to shoulder in resisting attempts to measure the effectiveness of their work. In situations where we've encountered this level of distrust, we don't introduce learning loops right away. We go back to the practices described in the first four chapters of this book, and start there. Only with a foundation of trust in place can you begin to build learning loops. No amount of pressure will force people to learn—it has to be a choice made voluntarily.

Learning loops are only useful if people take time to share the information and discuss how to improve performance. This can be problematic when managers and team members from different departments get together. "Nine times out of ten," as one manager said, "the problems within our company result from the invisible barriers between departments." Managers who haven't communicated very well in the past are most likely to feel threatened by learning loops. They will refuse to disclose key data; they'll halfheartedly participate in brainstorming; in short, they'll find all sorts of excuses to refrain from engaging in the process. Yet the biggest gains in performance are going to occur across these departmental communication cracks.

The first sign of resistance will be around sharing the information across departments. People will decide to email the performance information without creating a forum to discuss it or learn from it. As a leader, you can't let this happen! People must talk in order to learn. Meetings should be held to build trust among the players. This investment in communication will be difficult for some people to swallow. Senior leaders need to visibly support the process and highlight the dividends. They need to continually champion the process and show the linkage between learning loops and accelerating the pace of change.

Leaders also need to model the kinds of discussions that should take place: they need to ask tough questions, look under rocks, and ask why things aren't the way they expect them to be. Here are a few examples of the tough questions we like to see:

- "What activities do we currently engage in that consume a lot of resources but have little impact on our performance?"
- "What activities have the greatest impact on performance but are underresourced?"
- "If we were forced, how could we achieve another five percent improvement? How about ten percent?"

- "What are the gaps between our departments that we could easily fix to improve communication?"
- "If we were together in one department, what would we be doing that we aren't doing now?"

MAKING LEARNING LOOPS WORK

Here are some additional considerations in making learning loops work.

Learning loops need to be immediate. People need to hear as quickly as possible what's going on. It's not good enough to have annual performance updates. It's not good enough to email the report or publicize it on a website. Teams need to get the information in close to real time, think through the implications, discuss options, and share ideas. Feedback needs to occur as soon as the information is available so that people can talk about it and figure out ways to adjust their business practices and improve. That's how learning loops work.

At CarMax, the chain of used-car superstores, former CEO Austin Ligon held regular sessions with employees and began by sharing the latest performance information. Then he would ask: "What are we doing that is stupid, unnecessary, or doesn't make sense? How can we improve our performance?" He personally took part in these brainstorming sessions and made sure every idea was recorded and received a response.

Learning loops should occur throughout the organization. Don't limit them to the senior leadership team. Frontline teams need to be talking about which targets are being met—and which are not. Frontline supervisors should be given the information as soon as it's available and share it with their teams. Ideas for improvement need to bubble up. Every supervisor and manager should champion the learning loop process. Supervisors who are not sharing the data and facilitating good discussions need to be coached. Those who consistently fail to support learning loops need to be weeded out.

At a global IT solutions company, the CEO requires his senior leaders to attend a monthly meeting to review performance. Each leader has to explain what he or she learned in the last month—and how that learning is influencing their approach to the business. Large charts display the most recent data related to on-time delivery, change requests, adherence to budget, and customer complaints. And it gets results! Managers can no longer cover up their inadequacies or blame anyone else because everyone is in the room.

Successful ideas for improvement that emerge from the learning loop process should be documented and broadcast across the organization, so that everyone has a sense that things are happening, atoms are in motion, the pace of change is accelerating. At one of our client's companies, the division manager does a monthly video highlighting people's suggestions, stressing ideas that have resulted in significant improvement.

Learning loops should be composed both of "forward" indicators as well as "lagging" indicators. Achieving a given financial target is a lagging indicator of performance, since there's little predictive value in the results. Forward indicators might be things like marketing data showing which customers are buying new products, or data showing that people are feeling more positive about your company. Customer behavior data is one of the best forward-looking indicators. At a chain of auto parts stores in the western United States, store managers are measured on how often customers provide feedback of any kind. The idea? "We want to encourage managers to figure out ways to get feedback, so they can learn what our customers think," says CEO Greg Dunn. "If that means they go out and openly solicit it, that's fine. We want that dialogue with customers."

Disgruntled customers can give you a headache, but they can also give you an earful of good information. At W. L. Gore, makers of Gore-Tex products, managers are required to meet with customers once a month to discuss what they're seeing. The information is immediately shared with employees, who are asked to dig deeper, discover the underlying causes, and make things better.

When they're designed right, learning loops should stimulate change naturally. Think about what happens when you're speeding down the freeway and see a police car in your rearview mirror. Your brain compares the data on your speedometer to the posted speed limit—and sends an immediate message to your foot to slow down. All of this happens in less than a second. In other words, data related to performance has been shared immediately with the people empowered to improve it!

When managed well, the experience of seeing learning loops in action is itself a learning loop for people who are slow to get on board.

They see that conversations are taking place, information is being openly shared, and change is happening. They recognize a simple truth: if they don't get on board, they could get the equivalent of an organizational speeding ticket!

Human beings learn very quickly if they have information at their disposal and are motivated to improve performance. The philosopher Eric Hoffer put it this way: "In times of change, *learners* inherit the world, while the *learned* remain beautifully equipped to deal with a world that no longer exists."[2]

A Tibetan proverb says, "To be uncertain is uncomfortable. To be certain is foolish." Leaders who build learning loops enable the organization to focus on continual learning and improvement. It may be uncomfortable sometimes, but that focus on learning is what generates trust and builds a high-performing organization.

IGNORANCE LOOPS

The opposite of learning loops are ignorance loops. They occur when people assume they know the answers—and avoid looking further. If their assumptions aren't challenged, the result is an "ignorance loop": a feedback system that reinforces ignorance rather than intelligence.

The diagram on this page shows an ignorance loop in action. In this case, a chief executive is trying to deal with the fact that sales are down—and so he fires his sales manager. When sales remain down, he defends his decision to fire the sales manager by saying the product must be at fault. He then fires the product manager! In other words, he's no longer listening to the data; he's defending his decision. The cycle continues until someone intervenes with better data and communication to break the cycle.

Ignorance loops are born of the fact that once we make a decision, we select data and evidence that backs up our decision. We are hardwired to selectively sort information that reinforces our "rightness." This principle of cognitive dissonance is well known to psychologists. Once we buy a house or a car, no matter what the price, we select data to support the notion that we made a good deal. Unless we are highly attuned to our assumptions, we'll ignore data that suggests we made a bad decision (unless or until the evidence becomes overwhelming).

IGNORANCE LOOP

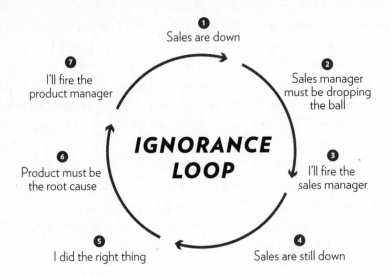

One of the biggest challenges a leader faces is weeding out ignorance loops. When Reg Murphy was CEO of National Geographic, he would hold regular Friday morning meetings with his management team. The purpose was to challenge people's thinking. Reg instructed his senior executives to come ready to learn—no matter how challenging the learning might be. The operating rule was to "talk about what we know this week that we didn't know last week."

People learned quickly that they had to bring hard data to these meetings—not their assumptions. They discussed marketing data, financial performance, and competitive trends. People were strongly discouraged from expressing any opinions about what the data meant until all the information had been shared.

In his way, Reg Murphy was instilling a new culture at National Geographic. He had observed a tendency for some personalities to prevail over others. He knew that if National Geographic were to successfully move into new ventures, he needed to substitute personality-driven "ignorance loops" with learning loops.

Here are some clues that you've stumbled onto an ignorance loop:

- "We can't afford to hire the best people."
- "We need to conserve our cash; we cannot afford this new program."
- "Even though this promotion didn't work last time, we think it will this time."
- "We are boxed in by our competitors and cannot change how we are positioned."
- "In order to meet this deadline, errors are unavoidable."

Wherever you look, you'll find examples of ignorance loops that reinforce mediocre performance. As I pointed out in the last chapter, research has shown that people assume themselves to be more competent than they actually are. Whether it's driving a car, navigating a new job, or playing a game, research has shown we trick ourselves into believing that we're doing a better job than we actually are. It is part of our fate as human beings to be forever chasing ourselves and our assumptions. But it's an important point. Our assumptions color our world. They magnify certain facets of our experience and filter through everything we say and do. We are our assumptions—at least at a cognitive level—and they are us.

How can you counter ignorance loops? The best way to confront them is with lots of good learning loops! If an R&D team is having a tough time developing new products, ask them to form a user group—and meet with it regularly. If the head of marketing says there's no way to improve your market share, ask her to meet with your largest customers first, inquire what the company could do to increase their share of business, and then formulate a plan to increase market share. Challenge people's assumptions. Ask "what if" questions to get them to think creatively. Ask them to talk to customers. Get them to collect objective data.

When ignorance loops are tolerated, people quickly lose the ability to think clearly. "Groupthink" begins to take over. Strange assumptions begin to assert themselves. For example, the CEO of a biotech company liked to go on long bicycle rides every Saturday. He invited others to join him, and as a result, several senior managers assumed the CEO liked people who were also into cycling. His top lieutenants spent thousands of dollars on cycling gear because they were all vying for his attention—and promotions. In fact, it became known inside the company that joining the "Spinners

Club" was important for getting promoted. Imagine everyone's surprise, then, when the CEO picked someone outside the Spinners Club to be his successor. "I just felt we needed an injection of new blood," he said.

Here's another example: The three owners of an office supply company wanted to foster a close-knit, family culture in their organization. In order to do so, they hired a consultant who encouraged them to form employee teams in four different areas: marketing, human resources, merchandising, and sales.

These teams met monthly. When Marketing wanted to produce a new brochure, the marketing team had to agree before it went to press. When Merchandising wanted to add a new product, the merchandising team had to reach consensus. When Human Resources wanted to set up a mentoring program, the team designed the program. People seemed happy to be involved. The owners felt glad that they had created such a close, family culture.

Then a competitor moved in. The company lost three customers, then four, then five. The owners assembled the teams. What to do? "Run it through the marketing team," someone suggested. But the marketing team didn't know what to do. The owners huddled. They didn't know what to do either. They couldn't decide.

So they hired a new consultant. This time it was our firm. We did a situation assessment. It became quickly apparent that an ignorance loop was at work. Everyone thought: "We can only make decisions by reaching consensus among our teams. If we don't reach consensus, then we can't move ahead."

Over a twelve-month period we helped this company orchestrate a shift in culture. The company disbanded the teams, inserted new managers in major roles, and got rid of the consensus culture. In its place we began building a different kind of culture. A strategic plan put the focus on expanding the firm's suite of services. Delegations were clarified; learning loops were initiated. Within two years, the firm's revenues and profits hit new highs.

And the employees? Internal surveys showed they were much happier now that people's responsibilities were clear and they weren't wasting so much time in meetings!

HIDDEN LEARNING LOOPS

Every organization has what we call "hidden learning loops." These are networks of information that send powerful signals to employees. Who has access to the boss? Whose budget is protected? Whose ego is prickly? Patterns like these send powerful messages—and create hidden learning loops in the organization.

Consider the question of status. People are always looking for cues about where they stand in relation to one another. Ancient cultures communicated their status with amulets and jewelry. In modern organizations, people communicate their status by their level of access to the boss. Effective leaders, who want to build high-performing organizations, understand this quest for status and deal with it in the following way.

First, they demonstrate their accessibility. They move out of the corner office with a secretary sitting guard and design physical layouts that send a clear message: "Everyone is on the same team here."

Once they're out in the open, they make physical contact with everyone. Great leaders don't hide behind their email or limit "face time" to a single meeting per week. Instead, they walk the floors, talk to different people, ask how things are going, and talk about ideas for improvement. In the process, they're letting everyone know: "My door is open. If you have something you want to talk about, come see me."

Going further, they strip away unnecessary trappings of status. Private dining rooms, special parking garages, and executive elevators symbolize an "us against them" idea of management.

Here are some of the hidden learning loops to watch out for:

- **Human resources:** Are salary ranges equivalent for similar jobs in different departments?
- **Capital resources:** Who gets the newest computers? The best desks?
- **Titles:** How are titles distributed? Are they even necessary?
- **Office layout:** Who's closest to the boss? Does it make sense? Should you rotate people in and out?
- **Office space:** Who gets a private office? Should you even have offices?

- **Dining rooms:** Is it really necessary to have an executive dining room?
- **Clubs:** Who has access? Why?
- **Dress code:** Does everyone wear the same uniform?
- **Access to financial information:** Who sees profit and loss statements? Why doesn't everybody?

In essence, each of these examples is a hidden learning loop that reinforces the idea that some people are better than others, or more entitled than others. These kinds of learning loops send powerful messages—and they may not be the messages you want your organization to hear.

CHANGE THE TRUST EQUATION

Some people are inherently reluctant to change. Others embrace it. To accelerate the pace of change, you may need to change "the trust equation."

In the introduction, I talked about how trust hinges on predictable expectations. If I do something for you, then I expect to get something in return. That's the principle of reciprocal altruism. It's at the root of trust. Changing the trust equation means animating the workplace with mechanisms of reciprocity that encourage change, rather than subvert it.

First and foremost, people need to believe that the change will result in an overall improvement in the way the company does business. At Apple, what drove its momentous growth was a relentless focus on the user. CEO Steve Jobs created a culture that continuously experimented with new ways to surprise and delight customers.

Intel is another company with a relentless focus on change. With each new project, employees compete for positions on project teams. Those who bring the best ideas and proven skills get selected. Those who get left out are literally left without jobs. It's "survival of the fittest," and it creates a culture of continuous improvement, innovation, and success at Intel.

In the end, the most powerful way to accelerate the pace of change is to engage people in real, honest discussions. Once people understand why continuous change is truly important for the company's future success, it ignites a sense of ownership. This has nothing to do with compensation and everything to do with instilling a sense of purpose. Once people see what is truly essential for the company's success, it unleashes the natural drive to improve.

With that idea in mind, it is the leader's job to make sure this honest conversation is taking place regularly throughout the organization. That means reorienting yourself to see that building systems of communication is the most important thing you can do.

THREE LEVELS OF CHANGE

Change happens at different levels of the organization: the strategic level, the process level, and the people level. Companies that accelerate change at all three levels will outperform everyone else—hands down!

ACCELERATING CHANGE AT THREE LEVELS

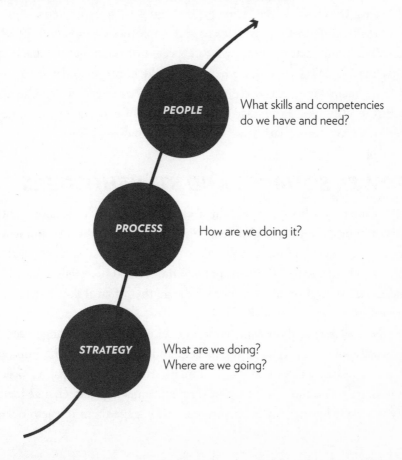

PEOPLE — What skills and competencies do we have and need?

PROCESS — How are we doing it?

STRATEGY — What are we doing? Where are we going?

At the strategic level, leaders should be continuously scrutinizing the environment and determining how best to capitalize on strengths and opportunities, how to minimize weaknesses and threats, and how to prepare for possible disruptions to their business model. They should be having honest, open discussions about how best to deploy resources to take advantage of opportunities and counter any threats. They should be setting clear priorities about how to best serve their customers, and making the needed adjustment in terms of services, products, business lines, organizational capacity, and structure.

At the process level, people should be honing processes to be sure they are as effective and efficient as possible. They should be monitoring performance and making adjustments to improve quality, reduce cycle time, and optimize the use of resources. There is a clear set of steps that we take each time we engage with our clients to help them hone their processes. The chart on the facing page captures these eight steps.

Finally, at the people level, teams and employees should continuously receive communication about what's expected of them, get feedback on what they're doing well and what they could improve, and receive the training, mentoring, and coaching they need to be more effective. Change at this level hinges on regular communication of expectations, frequent feedback (both appreciative and constructive), and coaching.

POWER SOURCES AND STAKEHOLDERS

In considering who to engage in a change process, think about both "power sources" and "stakeholders." *Power sources* are the key influencers in your organization, the people who control the resources needed to make change work. They can provide money and materials, education and expertise, and political support. Engage them first if you want to be successful.

Stakeholders are those who stand to gain or lose if the change occurs. Internally, these are typically managers and employees in the affected areas. Externally, they may be customers, consumer groups, advocacy groups, partners, and other suppliers. Effective managers of change identify the likely losers early in the process and engage them in the process.

If this doesn't work, then they try to neutralize their effectiveness. Finding other influential champions who can control or mute their voices can be of great assistance. When stakeholders are organized and carry a lot of clout, such as unions, engaging them early on and making them part of the process is vital to success.

KEY STEPS OF PROCESS IMPROVEMENT

STEP	KEY PRACTICES
1. Examine your processes in light of your core values, purpose, and vision.	Don't start until you have a good strategic focus in place.
2. Define the result you want and the rationales for change.	Be sure to communicate these things publically to all affected. This begins the alignment.
3. Make sure there's a clear champion or group of champions.	Champions are always needed to break down resistance to change.
4. Define the sequence of deliverables: where you expect to be and when.	Don't begin the journey until you know where you're going.
5. Make sure the resources are adequate to do the job well.	Don't discount the value of expert consultants. They'll help you get there faster and with less pain.
6. Appoint a planning group to do the work and own the work.	Let those who own the work decide whether to refine, reengineer, or eliminate the process in consultation with the champions.
7. Let measurable criteria drive the success of the new process.	You are what you measure. Tie the process to measures of customer satisfaction, cost, revenue, and/or profit.
8. Communicate your progress along the way.	Make sure you continue to align the organization by telling people what's happening and what's going to change.

MANAGING SUCCESSFUL CHANGE

This chapter is all about change. So far, I've focused on how to use learning loops to accelerate organic change from within. I would be remiss, in a chapter about change, if I didn't also talk about the techniques to manage broad organizational change successfully. How do you engage an entire organization in effectively moving from one way of thinking about the business to another? How do you drive strategy from the top of the organization so that it is supported and implemented throughout? How do you optimize the change process?

There are seven stages to a successful change process, as the following figure illustrates. Let's take a closer look at each stage.

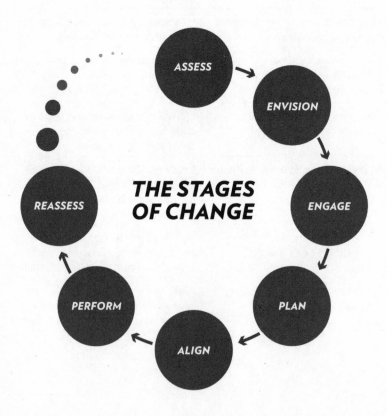

1. **Assess the current state.** The first step in any change process is to agree on a set of reasons why the status quo is unacceptable. As you articulate why the status quo is unacceptable, translate those findings into rationales for change. For example, if your declining market share is unacceptable, then the rationale for change is to regain a dominant market position. Company leaders need to fully endorse this rationale.

2. **Envision the desirable future.** The next step is to envision the future you want. Your vision should be a win-win, both for your customers and for the company's performance. If an organization-wide change is envisioned, this vision must come from the CEO and senior management.

3. **Engage people in change.** The third step is to engage managers and staff in planning how to implement the change. The planning process should start with key managers. It may need to cascade all the way down to the front lines.

4. **Put the plan in writing.** The fourth step is to develop a written plan, documenting the strategies and action steps that are needed for implementing the desired change. This document needs to be broadly endorsed and championed by the company's leadership.

5. **Align people around the plan.** Once senior leaders have approved the plan, make sure everyone understands the specific strategies for change. Communicate up, down, and across the organization. Managers play a critical role in this communication—a fact too often forgotten in the haste toward implementation. Every affected manager needs to champion the change.

6. **Perform according to plan.** During this phase, people must work to achieve the objectives of the plan. Make sure learning loops are in place so that people can track whether the plan results in the desired effects. If the envisioned outcome is additional sales, are sales increasing? If the envisioned outcome is cost savings, make sure people are able to track those savings.

7. **Assess the results, then reassess your position.** During this final phase, you need to assess results. You should track both the desired outcomes and also the unseen and unintended consequences. For example, when one of our clients reengineered its sales process, it was envisioned that it would reduce overall costs to the company. But a follow-up analysis showed that the costs had not gone away—they'd only been shifted to other departments. The management team spent considerable time analyzing exactly which savings were real—and which were a mirage.

That's the change process in a nutshell. Now let's look at some of the key factors of success.

KEY FACTOR: ASSEMBLE A STRONG PLANNING TEAM

Key to effective change is assembling an influential and effective planning group that represents a broad cross section of interests. I already talked about power sources and stakeholders. Don't make the group too large. Ten to thirteen people is ideal. More than that, and it's difficult to have everyone feel engaged and taking part in the conversation.

When you're assembling the team, here are a few other factors to consider aside from their level of authority and influence:

- **A mixture of viewpoints**—People who are deeply familiar with the issue should be combined with people who have less of a stake in the solution.

- **Representation**—You want good representation from throughout the organization so that no one with a major stake in the outcome can challenge the process by saying: "You had no one on the team who represented us."

- **Skill in group process**—Choose people who have shown they can take the time to listen and understand other people's views, as well as be thoughtful advocates of their own position.

- **Mixture of communication styles**—Choose people who are analytical along with people who are more intuitive.[3] Choose a few assertive voices, but balance them with people who are more inquisitive.

KEY FACTOR: MANAGE THE DECISION PROCESS

Once the team is in place, members need to decide on their rules of engagement and make sure they fully understand the overall decision-making process—and their role in it—before they begin actual work. As I discussed in Chapter 4, it's critical that the planning team's decision-making responsibilities are clear. Otherwise, you'll wind up with a change process that no one understands and is cumbersome to track and manage.

Is the team's role to develop detailed proposals to present to senior management for approval? Does the team have to reach consensus? Does it have the final say? Who will make the ultimate call? The board of directors? The CEO? Some other manager or management team? Make sure decision-making roles are clear.

KEY FACTOR: PROVIDE THE NECESSARY TIME

The head of a major government agency reacted with surprise when we told him it would take six months for his organization to develop a strategic plan. "All I want is for people to know their goals," he said. "Why should it take so long?"

Real change takes time. It requires time for people to analyze and decide on the organization's priorities. People need to process complex data and develop different scenarios. They need to build agreement for a particular set of actions. The investment in time will be returned tenfold in the durability of the commitments and attention to results you get down the road.

KEY FACTOR: HIRE A SKILLED FACILITATOR

An obvious reason to hire a skilled facilitator is to make sure the discussion stays on track and that everyone's ideas are heard. Members of the planning group should carefully weigh the merits of choosing one of the group's members to facilitate. The facilitator needs to be neutral, and needs to be unhampered by fears of losing his or her job. An outside facilitator can bring neutrality and a wealth of experience to the process. This creates a positive climate of trust in which people feel free to express their viewpoints.

A skilled facilitator can also help make sure you design an effective change process. Much as a ship's navigator helps chart the course, a skilled facilitator should be able to help you achieve the right balance of engagement and speed. The facilitator should be able to orient the group at all times—and put each step in the journey into context.

A skilled facilitator should also help you capture the most important ideas and organize them. Ultimately, he or she should be able to help you draft documents, such as a strategic plan or action plan.

KEY FACTOR: FOCUS ON A FEW PRIORITIES

Most people and most organizations can only absorb one or two large change initiatives at one time. When managing a change process, focus on one, two, or three priorities. Leave the rest for later.

The best way to identify priorities is to first do a light analysis to see whether a particular goal or priority rises to the top. If the light analysis doesn't reveal the best option, do a deeper analysis. The planning group should ask: What are the costs and benefits of implementing each option we're considering? What will have the greatest impact on our customers and our long-term success at the least cost? You don't need a detailed cost-benefit analysis; you need a reasonable estimate—enough to be able to see which option has the greatest merit.

THE IMPACT MATRIX

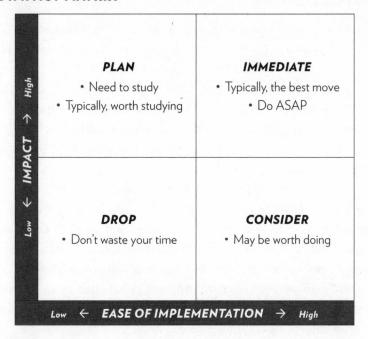

KEY FACTOR: KEEP AN EYE ON YOUR CHAMPIONS

The ongoing support and championship of the leaders in the organization is crucial to any change process. If the planning group encounters resistance, then the top leader's authority needs to be invoked. What if the champions start to wilt at this moment? Then the planning group should either wait until new champions appear—or disband. Championship from the top is essential if change is going to be real and meaningful. If the champions have vanished, there's no point in proceeding.

• • •

CONCLUSION

The genius of the reciprocating engine lies in the cyclical action of the piston and cylinder. Each downward stroke exerts force on the piston rod while drawing fuel into the cylinder for the next cycle. The genius of learning organizations is creating an engine of accelerating change. The downward stroke, if you like, is the delivery of value to customers, while at the same time the downward motion sucks information and intelligence from customers into the organization—to be digested by it immediately for the next cycle.

The point is simple: the key to high performance is creating learning loops that energize the creative process. The best learning loops are like brains, taking in data, responding to pressures, and above all continuously learning and adapting. While the notion is simple, it is difficult to pull off—especially in an organization where turf wars or political jealousies may cause managers to hoard information rather than share it. This can pose the greatest challenge for an organization—but it is also one of the most rewarding things that a leader can do.

Just as we are always becoming leaders, we are always in the midst of change. As a leader, your challenge is to make everyone in the organization a part of this dynamic to accelerate the pace of change. Sometimes it requires burning the bridges—tearing down a symbolic vestige of the old organization. Sometimes, as at Intel, it means telling people they have to join a new team, invent a new job, or leave. Often it means getting people to talk about issues they may initially not want to talk about.

Above all, accelerating the pace of change requires managing yourself differently. It means becoming increasingly aware of your own strengths and weaknesses—and learning the painful truth that you need to act in new ways in order to build trust and spark innovation.

STIMULATE CREATIVE FLOW

$$(ACV+STF+LTO+MDW+SWY) + (APC+SCF+SST+MTC+APQ) = LC$$

In 2003, a team of four hundred employees from Sutter Hospital in Northern California launched a drive to win a Malcolm Baldrige National Quality Award. Led by Janet Wagner, the hospital's chief administrative officer, the team began by asking: "What is it that we do best? What do we want to excel at? What's our core competency?" They concluded that it was their "culture of caring, how we take care of each other, our patients, our doctors, our community."

Janet brought in a team of consultants to help them develop a set of specific behaviors tied to the culture of caring. But the project hit an obstacle. One of the night nurses came to Wagner and said: "I don't think my colleagues are getting it." Wagner asked her to elaborate. "Sometimes senior management talks about things and rolls them out, and they don't really connect [the dots] with every single frontline employee."

Wagner reevaluated. She asked the night nurse, Carolyn Campos, if she would work with her employees to customize the behaviors. Carolyn agreed, and instead of six behaviors, Carolyn and her staff came up with ten. Carolyn then developed a training module for all frontline employees to help spark their understanding. Nurses practiced the desired behaviors to the point that they became second nature. As an example of how this approach stimulated a wholesale change in employee behavior, Wagner tells the story of a patient in the intensive care unit who was dying. Her dream was to see a European garden, but the nursing staff knew she wasn't going to make it. So they brought the patient books filled with pictures of European gardens, to surround her with images of the things she loved.

PRACTICE #7:
STIMULATE CREATIVE FLOW

....

Effective leaders understand the connection between work and happiness—and create workplaces in which people are encouraged to innovate and tap their creative flow. In a leadership culture, people are entrusted with responsibility and expected to get things done. They feel supported to try new things—and are not micromanaged. When you stimulate creative flow, people stretch beyond their "safety" zones and tap hidden wells of personal talent and energy. They apply creative thinking to problem solving and achieve significant results in remarkably short periods of time.

Ten years after she launched the project, Janet Wagner and her team won the Baldrige Award. While that was the goal, Wagner says the experience taught her something more important: the need to connect with employees' belief systems and establish a framework for continuous improvement, all of it with the goal of stimulating creative flow.

THE DYNAMICS OF INNOVATION

This chapter gets at the roots of innovation. As you should know by now, half of the practices in the leadership equation focus on building trust, and half focus on sparking innovation. Innovation occurs when people feel their work is fulfilling to them. Innovation occurs when people are focused on achieving an important goal. Innovation occurs when people have the ability to control what they do and when they do it. Innovation occurs when managers reward people for ideas—and do not squelch them. Innovation occurs when people feel loose, speak freely, and are able to challenge orthodoxy.

Now if you look at this list, it bears an uncanny resemblance to the forces at work when people achieve what psychologists call "flow." Each of the things I mentioned—being intensely focused, controlling what you do, feeling loose, feeling fulfilled—are precursors to achieving flow. Over the years, I've concluded that a significant part of what managers and leaders do to spark innovation is to create an environment where people can easily experience "flow."

For many people, the word "flow" may strike them as odd. But I've been focused on it ever since I read the book *Flow: The Psychology of Optimal Experience* by Mihaly Csikszentmihalyi.[1] The author (his name is pronounced "six-cent-me-holly") describes flow as a mental state in which you feel fully immersed in what you are doing. It can occur in any field, in any industry, at any level. It is the feeling that you're doing exactly what you like doing—and what you're *meant* to be doing—whether it's designing software, selling shoes, or teaching a yoga class. In a word, it's the feeling that your work is *fulfilling*.

Csikszentmihalyi presents a compelling case that every human being is capable of and wants to maximize feelings of flow, and he identifies six factors that are necessary to achieve it. These factors can appear independently, but it is the combination that results in the flow experience:

1. You feel personal control over the situation or activity.
2. You experience the activity as intrinsically rewarding.
3. You concentrate intensely on the activity in the present moment.
4. You are so absorbed that you lose reflective self-consciousness.
5. Time appears to pass quickly.
6. Your actions and awareness are merged.

People feel happiest when they are in a state of flow, just as they are happiest when they experience feelings of trust. That's the genesis of the leadership equation. When these six factors come together, the alchemy is palpable: You feel your talents and abilities are being fully tapped. You feel like your life has meaning and authenticity. People who find flow in their jobs are genuinely amazed that they are being paid to do what they enjoy. It's not work when you love what you do.

This is true particularly in America, where we place such a high value on the work we do. Work is central to our sense of who we are. The flexible labor markets and upward mobility we enjoy have led to a universal feeling in America that working hard, and doing meaningful work, are keys to our happiness. What could be more important then, as a manager or a leader, than to create a workplace in which people are consistently able to achieve the peak experience of flow?

By the way, the data about happiness supports this conclusion. Americans who feel successful at work are twice as likely as people who don't feel that way to say they are very happy overall.[2] This isn't connected to money. Economists like the Nobel Prize winner Daniel Kahneman have demonstrated that once people have enough money to meet their needs, a big financial windfall has only a transitory impact on happiness. Long-term happiness depends on having a sense of success at work. Again, this is why helping people achieve creative flow is so important. Franklin Roosevelt put it this way: "Happiness lies not in the mere possession of money; it lies in the joy of achievement, in the thrill of creative effort."

EXAMPLES OF FLOW

Creative flow can occur in any profession. People doing routine, repetitive tasks can achieve creative flow; people engaged in highly competitive activity can achieve creative flow. Any type of work, when done well, requires the doer to focus, to think, to improve—in short, to engage in creative effort. I enjoy watching professional basketball, especially teams that play unselfishly and move the ball snappily around the court. It's the extra pass that creates both winning players and winning teams. "Our coach gives us the freedom to play loose and make plays, and guys aren't abusing it," is the way one player describes it. "Our team chemistry is unreal."

Brooks Robinson, the all-star third baseman of the Baltimore Orioles, described how he felt in flow during a game. He called it being "on." He knew without thinking when the ball was coming to him. He would react instantly to a line drive, grab the ball with his glove outstretched, twirl and throw to first, and make a tough play look easy. Robinson's skills generated an infectious winning chemistry that inspired other players on his team. Call it leadership, call it flow—but Brooks Robinson and the Orioles had it.

When I was twenty-one, I was part of a team of U.S. Forest Service firefighters called "hot shots." We were a rapid response team, flown in by helicopter to fight forest fires in the mountains of California. We trained hard. The work was dangerous, grueling, sometimes tedious, and also exhilarating. I was often in a state of flow, knowing we were doing something important and that each member of our team had an important role to play.

What was the key to our chemistry? It began with our boss, Gary. He was a humble, straightforward guy, who constantly taught us new skills and drilled us to handle all kinds of fire situations. He also focused on finding out what each of us enjoyed doing. When he learned that I was good with carpentry, he assigned me the role of renovating our barracks and workshop. Like any good coach, he knew when to give direction and when to stand back and let us try things on our own. Thanks to Gary, our team of firefighters had flow.

HOW TO STIMULATE FLOW

As a leader and manager, how do you spark creative flow in other people? I think there are five keys.

First, be clear about the goal. What does "winning" look like? Is it a certain initiative completed by a certain time? Is it a given number of sales? Is it a completed assignment? Define the goal well and you've provided people the opportunity to experience flow.

Second, make sure the goal is achievable. If it's outside people's control, if it's beyond their capabilities, if they don't have the resources to get it done, then you've not set them up to achieve flow. Ask what resources they need and keep asking these questions: "Do you have the resources you need?" "Do you think you can get this done?" "Can you overcome the challenges?" If you hear a no to any of these questions, recalibrate the goal. Don't expect to get the best out of people in the quest of the impossible— or even the improbable.

Third, provide people the freedom to figure it out. Let's talk about this for a moment. One of the myths of management is that good managers vigilantly track what people are doing. In fact, good managers set clear goals and expectations and then let people figure out how to get it done. As General George Patton put it: "Don't tell people how to do things. Tell them *what* to do and let them surprise you with their results."[3] For example, at our leadership academy, we assign leadership projects to teams of five to seven people. We explain what each team needs to do—that all teams need to scope their project, do the necessary research, and present their recommendations to their CEO. We provide them coaching as they request it, but we don't track their progress. We assume that these are adults who fully understand the consequences should they fail to make a good presentation to their CEO.

Fourth, put people together who truly enjoy each other's company. In Chapter 3, I stressed the importance of hiring people who mesh well and who uphold your company's core values. Your job as a leader and manager is to get the right players on the court, people who look forward to seeing each other every day and who want to work together collaboratively. This is a case where one bad apple truly will spoil the barrel. If you do nothing else, pay attention to the chemistry, and if you see it's not working, figure out a new way to mix people together. This is a problem that won't fix itself.

Fifth, make people feel good about what they're doing. Criticism comes easy; praise comes hard. But it's the praise that works magic—especially praise for the actual work people do. To express appreciation for specific things that another person has done takes all of five minutes. But those five minutes are remembered for days, even weeks. My rule of thumb is this: give ten times as much praise as criticism. When you do, people will hear your criticism as a genuine desire to help them improve. Be particularly attentive to the people you work with most often, because you will tend to take them for granted. Moreover, count to ten before saying no to their ideas. Being too quick on the trigger will kill innovation.

Coaching and empowerment inspire flow. Praise inspires flow. Good teamwork inspires flow. Micromanagement kills flow. Good managers invest the time to get to know people, find out what's important to them, and discover what they enjoy doing. They provide a work environment in which experimentation is encouraged and communication is strong. As people do well, they get positive feedback, both from within themselves and from others. This feeling of excellence helps spark further feelings of innovation and flow. That virtuous cycle is what you're aiming for.

At the outset of Southwest Airlines' remarkable growth, CEO Herb Kelleher focused on finding people who excelled at being "people" people. As a result, flying on Southwest became fun. Flight attendants telling jokes, singing songs, and engaging passengers in mid-air trivia contests—this became part of the Southwest experience. Southwest's investment in its people paid off when it came time to negotiate with the airline's unions. Southwest had invested heavily in a ratio of one supervisor for every ten employees, a tight ratio in an industry where the norm was one to twenty. When Southwest needed to negotiate a new compensation agreement with its unions, the investment paid off: Southwest experienced no work stoppages.

Technology companies in Silicon Valley invest heavily in helping their employees experience creative flow. At Apple, software engineers pick their own projects to work on. Apple sees this as paying a double dividend: first, it helps the company retain its corps of talented engineers; second, it results in innovations that can further catalyze the company's growth. Facebook is another company that puts a premium on providing employees the freedom to work on projects they choose. Engineers get a regular day off to pursue whatever project they feel like.

One of the operations managers at GlaxoSmithKline's research facility in Palo Alto spends a day each year with each of his employees. "I want to discover what you like to do," he tells them, "and what you want to get out of life and your work." People spend the day with him, talking about life and career goals. He then tries to find new projects that tap into what people like to do. Needless to say, his employees feel highly supported. The company's track record of retaining key employees backs it up.

When we survey leaders, however, many of them say they spend too little time helping employees tap their creative energies. So ask yourself: "When do I experience flow? What could I do to make my work more fulfilling to me? And what could I do to inspire flow in others more often?"

THE DYNAMICS OF FEAR

Creative flow happens when people aren't feeling afraid—afraid of losing their jobs, scared of losing status, scared of being left out, afraid of being punished. The dynamics of fear can be asphyxiating to an organization.

Who's responsible for eliminating fear? You are! I make it a habit to ask our employees: Is there anything at work that causes you fear? If the answer is yes, I do my best to eliminate it. A young college graduate who'd recently joined our company once told me: "I'm afraid of losing my job." I asked him: "If I guarantee you your job for a year, how would that change how you approach working here?" He said it would make him feel much more focused and committed. I said: "Fine, so long as you don't do anything to embarrass the company, the job is yours for a year." That young man rose to be a senior vice president. Today he laughs when I remind him of his early fears.

Fun is the natural antidote to fear. Fun helps people relax, be themselves, and speak their minds. At Wal-Mart's headquarters in Arkansas, weekly staff meetings begin with a cheer conceived by founder Sam Walton. To understand this story, you have to know that the punctuation mark in Wal-Mart's name is called the "squiggly." The cheer starts with the traditional "Give me a W . . ." When they come to the squiggly, everyone shakes their bottoms.

So ask yourself: Do I encourage people to relax and have fun? Do I make a point of driving out fear? Do I provide opportunities for people to let down their hair and laugh together? If you're answering no, you're probably not doing everything you can to encourage flow.

FLOW AND THE WORKSPACE

Another factor of flow is the physical workspace itself. The offices of Synergex, a software company in Northern California, have special "think rooms" with soft pillows where team meetings can take place. There are no offices—only low dividers between desks. The emphasis on open communication has paid off in the morale, creativity, and growth of the organization.

At the Washington D.C. offices of a large lobbying firm, people work in open spaces, separated by low dividers that allow outside light to spill into every corner. Informal meeting spaces with colorful chairs and tables dot the office. Morale is high. And people feel creative. When there are no walls, no dividers, and no offices, it's much easier for people to communicate and share ideas.

So ask yourself: Am I doing everything I can to create an environment in which communication can flow easily? Is there plenty of natural light? Is everyone able to see each other? Are there plenty of spaces where people can meet informally to solve problems? If the answer is no, then you're probably not tapping into people's creative flow.

BALANCE SELF-CONFIDENCE AND UNCERTAINTY

Here's another key to stimulating flow: uncertainty. In a recent study, managers were given a survey and asked to rate how many of their decisions each day were absolutely correct.[4] They were also asked to evaluate their level of confidence. Employees were then asked to assess their relationships with these managers.

BALANCING SELF-CONFIDENCE AND UNCERTAINTY

Here's what the research revealed: Managers who were confident but relatively *uncertain* were viewed as better managers, more likely to foster creative flow and encourage independent thinking. Those who were confident and *certain* were viewed as authoritarian and inflexible.

When you think about it, this conclusion isn't too surprising. When people work for leaders who are confident but *uncertain*, they feel more relaxed, more expressive, and more innovative. When you work for a boss who is confident and *certain*, you're left feeling that your own contributions aren't as important. You tend to feel second-guessed. Before you know it, most of your energy is devoted to managing your boss's reactions rather than to finding better ways of doing things. Too much certainty snuffs out the spark.

To break this cycle, leaders need to openly admit their uncertainty—to confess that they don't always know the answers, to state openly that they look to others to find solutions. Great leaders go one step further. They continually poke at their own assumptions and expose their "facts" as probabilities—not certainties. They encourage people to search for better solutions.

ENABLE LOCAL INVENTION

With rare exception, innovation and flow most often occur at a local level, meaning where small teams or individuals are trying to improve a specific service or product that is directly tied to their work. GE demonstrated this kind of thinking. In his now famous "workout meetings," CEO Jack Welch regularly asked employees to suggest ways to improve their local work process or business product. Welch put those employees' managers on the spot by saying they had three choices: accept the employee's idea on the spot, reject it on the spot (but only if they could justify their decision), or study it for ten days. If, after ten days, the manager still hadn't approved the innovation, it went into effect automatically.

Through his workout meetings, Welch let employees know that he valued their ideas—they had nothing to worry about if they came up with a better way of doing things or exposed inefficiencies. Workout meetings became powerful symbols of creative thinking and local invention at GE.

At Brøderbund, a California-based software maker, the senior product manager turned over the assignment of creating a new line of educational software to a team of young programmers. One of their first innovations was assembling a user group of eight-year-old girls and boys. Instead of relying on Brøderbund's point-and-click graphical interface, the team came up with an unconventional scheme that involved moving images and hidden buttons—resulting in a higher level of engagement and interest among younger users and higher levels of attained skills.

By taking advantage of local invention and bottom-up decision making, leaders encourage a form of behavior called "emergent intelligence." The theory of emergent intelligence reflects a growing field of research into how complex societies and organisms operate.

One of the principles of emergent intelligence is that organisms that operate under a few basic rules have an evolutionary advantage. Ant colonies are cited as a prime example. One rule of ants is that everyone but the queen is a multitasker. A second rule is: "Do what the ant next to you is doing." A third is for "outgoing foragers to give way to incoming ants carrying food." These three simple rules enable the colony to communicate and adapt to change very rapidly. One moment you take out the trash; the next you forage for food. Because they operate this way, ant colonies adapt quickly to change and thus survive.

The implications for encouraging innovation are profound. It suggests that simple rules might be very powerful when applied to people. At Intel, for example, once the year's initiatives are announced, people form into teams to do the work. But if a person doesn't land on a team within a fixed period of time, then he or she is fired. It's competitive, but it works. And creativity flourishes at Intel.

Dee Hock applied the principle of emergent intelligence when he engaged a team of bankers to create Visa in the 1970s. Up to that point, local banks had offered a variety of different credit cards—each with different rules. Hock and his team wanted to create a single credit card and clearing mechanism that would allow seamless financial transactions around the world.

Hock understood that banks needed to operate independently within well-understood rules. So his team worked hard for more than a year to define those rules. This was the genius of their process. The first rule they came up with was: "You keep what you earn." Banks that became Visa members would keep all but a tiny fraction of whatever fees or interest they generated.

The second rule was: "No limits on membership." Any bank was free to join the Visa alliance.

The third rule related to ownership. Since the banks needed the freedom to operate independently, no one should "own" Visa. Thus Visa was structured as a non-stock corporation with governance vested in the member banks. Since there was no stock, no single shareholder could gain a controlling interest in Visa.

The final rule related to management. A separate company would manage Visa's operations. But it would answer to a system of regional boards and to an executive board. Of the fees collected by the banks, a small fraction would go to this management company to take care of marketing, back-office operations, reconciliation, and so forth. But it would not be in a position to "control" Visa. The authority flowed the other way—from the member institutions. There was some fine print, but basically Visa was that simple. From those operating rules a worldwide form of currency was born.

From this experience, Hock invented the term "chaordic" organization. It reflects his belief that successful organizations walk a fine line between chaos and order. Order is represented by top-down decision making. Chaos is represented by bottom-up decision making. Chaordic organizations, in Hock's eyes, balance the two by having clear values, a well-defined vision, and sound operating principles. They also have clear ways to measure success. Within that framework, people are left to create strategies and devise solutions as they see fit. It is a model that is perfectly in keeping with sparking innovation, inspiring flow, and building a leadership culture.

RECOGNIZE SUCCESS

To encourage flow, good managers need to make sure people are recognized early on for their success. Every success should be recognized in some way, no matter how small. Rewards and praise should be distributed liberally, to all who were involved. At the same time, a special effort needs to be made to celebrate and recognize people who made special contributions.

I've already mentioned my 10:1 rule about the balance between positive feedback and critical or "constructive" feedback. People need to hear ten times more positive feedback than negative. Otherwise, they simply will not—or cannot—hear the constructive feedback. The "constructive" part of the feedback will be lost. By focusing on praise and encouragement, you can help prepare people for the day when they need to hear the constructive feedback.

Rewarding success is a key way to encourage people to develop into confident leaders who "run it like they own it." Our firm has developed a "Leadership Development Lifecycle" that illustrates the specific points in a leader's development. An important step is creating an Individual Development Plan, in which you write down your career goals and the kinds of training, mentoring, job shadowing, and feedback you need. Encouraging creative flow means giving people this opportunity to reflect on and articulate their career aspirations—and then share them with the people who can help them get there.

TURNING FAILURE INTO SUCCESS

Nobody fails because they make mistakes. Failure is only when people stop trying. Leaders should not frame mistakes as failures, but as learning points—inevitable steps on the path of innovation. Smart leaders know there's much to be learned from mistakes. We worked with a company that made software applications for medium-sized companies. Tom, the company's CEO, was a big, affable guy in his mid-forties and a very open communicator.

Tom wanted his software development team to create a new product that would dramatically simplify the use of Java tools. Yet Tom worried that the team had grown complacent and risk averse. "We don't know how to do that," one of his engineers grumbled when Tom announced the result he wanted. "That's all right," said Tom. "You'll learn."

Tom set up four teams inside the engineering department and gave them a deadline to come up with the new software product. On the wall he put four color-coded charts with milestones and timescales—one for each team. The process created a frenzy of activity. The teams worked like crazy. On the last day, they asked Tom to come into the conference room.

"We've got good news and we've got bad news," the engineering VP said.

Tom glanced up. "Tell me the good news first."

"We've got a heck of a product," said the department chief.

"And the bad news?" asked Tom.

"It doesn't work," said the engineer, "at least not yet."

Tom smiled. "Sounds great," he said. "Tell me more."

The engineers described the product and outlined for Tom how it would work—eventually, if given more time. Tom encouraged them to keep working at it. Four weeks later, the team came in with big grins on their faces. "Guess what?" they said. "It works better than we imagined!"

Today, that product is the backbone of the company's record profits.

FOSTERING HEALTHY COMPETITION

Fostering healthy competition can help stimulate creative flow. Rather than focus on individual competition, a smart strategy is to set up team competitions that fuel fun and innovation. As one manager says, "It is amazing how much people can get done if they don't worry about who gets the credit."

One of our clients promotes an annual competition among its teams. The CEO gets very involved in defining the competition. One year the goal was getting the highest rating for customer satisfaction. Another year, it was showing the greatest increase in productivity. The company sends the top-performing team members along with their families to some exotic locale. To promote the competition, the CEO posts pictures of tropical beaches in Costa Rica or Bora Bora around the office. Flyers describe midnight snorkel trips and beachside barbecues. At the end of the year, the top-performing team is selected. One year, every team performed well and the company enjoyed strong profits. So what did the CEO do? She shut down the company and flew everyone to Hawaii for a week.

BATTLE BUREAUCRATIC "CREEP"

Bureaucratic "creep" is the force that stands in direct opposition to innovation and creative flow. Bureaucratic creep starts when a manager feels he has to exert control over how something gets done. Perhaps he's been told to get it right "or it's your job." So he installs a new checkpoint to monitor a particular decision or set of decisions, or to monitor whether a given milestone has been achieved.

Each time a decision hits a checkpoint, it's reviewed. If it falls outside predetermined norms, it's rejected. The bureaucracy is unthinking about the quality of the exception—or the larger need for innovation. It only knows yes or no. It only knows how to exert control. The checkpoint becomes a choke point.

Over time, the new checkpoint becomes embedded in company policy. People are trained to adhere to it. As employees chafe under a system that demands decisions adhere to certain specifications, bureaucratic creep starts to drive away the more talented, innovative people. So the creative brain trust starts to erode. New employees are brought in who tend to be more mediocre. As the talent turns over, more mistakes occur.

Now the bureaucracy starts to flourish. It grows in order to exert control over increasing mediocrity and increasing numbers of errors. This further alienates the talented individuals. Before you know it, a culture of mediocrity has swept in. Like a virus, bureaucracy has fully taken over.

Smart managers are relentless in empowering people to figure out better ways to do things and make decisions on their own. They tolerate a level of chaos and uncertainty in order to preserve and encourage creative spark. Above all, they battle bureaucratic creep.

KEY FACTORS OF SUCCESSFUL INNOVATION

Innovation means letting people try things out to see if they will work. Often this means you've got to change your own behaviors as a manager. If a new program or product isn't to your liking, think twice before imposing your critical judgment on it. If people believe it will work, then embrace it and let people have a chance to prove themselves. It's easy to say you encourage dissent. But the true test lies in how other people perceive you. Ask someone:

1. "Do you think I'm open to fresh, new ways of doing things?"
2. "Do people feel free to speak their minds around me?"

3. "Are people afraid to try new things because of fear of what I might say or do?"

4. "In general, do I come across as judgmental and closed-minded? Or do I come across as open and curious?"

"Creative dissent stimulates me," says the executive at a large bank. "I have nothing to lose, and everything to gain, by people challenging the status quo." Only when people truly feel that their oddball ideas and schemes are welcome can it be said that you are creating an environment that sparks innovation and encourages creative flow.

Aside from the openness of leaders, what are some of the other factors behind successful innovation? First, and most obvious, you need to provide the resources to be innovative. In essence, this means not short-changing the creative process. Rather than starve a project, you need to find ways to do things cheaper, better, faster. Often this means beginning with a small pilot project, assessing success, and then investing additional resources.

Second, successful innovation is most often based on market demand. The "7-10 rule" states that historically seven out of ten successful innovations are driven by a recognizable customer need—rather than a new concept, technique, or technology seeking a need. So encourage people to get close to your markets and customers to determine how much demand there actually is for the proposed product or service.

At this juncture, let me stress that not all successful innovation is the result of market "pull." In fact, some of the most successful innovations are the result of market "push." Facebook and Twitter, to name two, are examples of products that customers did not know they needed until they were introduced.

A third factor of success is delegating the vast majority of both product and process innovation to individual divisions and departments. Empower groups of "dedicated fanatics"— small, self-managed teams that will carry the project forward regardless of the resistance they encounter.

A fourth factor of success is support at the senior management level. Senior managers who focus on failure are not going to encourage creative flow. A popular management saying is "Ready, fire, aim." It's silly, but it captures an important point: things won't be perfect the first time. The idea is to create flexible processes with learning loops built in, so that people can learn from their creative mistakes, adapt, and continually improve. Remember, don't frame well-intentioned mistakes as failures. Use them as learning moments.

Here are some more ways to encourage successful innovation:

- Create a corporate venture fund, with clear criteria for picking projects. Seed the fund with enough money to make people pay attention. Promote it and see what happens.

- Put together in-house teams to track your company's competitors, with each team focusing on one product or service niche. Hold regular brainstorming meetings for all teams to meet, share, and brainstorm products that would box out the competition.

- Send people from different levels of the organization to trade shows; create a regular forum for people to report on trade show highlights. Make sure that people from different departments attend.

- Create a new customer acquisition team. Charge the team with identifying and contacting one new customer each day.

- Form an advisory board consisting of people whom you'd most like to buy your products or services. Don't rest until they are your customers.

- Form an intern exchange program with a local university lab. Your employees work there for three months, while their students work at your company.

- Hold an offsite planning session dedicated to innovation. Hold it someplace where there are no chairs, and ask people to arrange the meeting space. Pose provocative questions, like: "What would we do differently if our two largest competitors merged?"

- Contact a business broker or investment banker. Tell them you're interested in acquiring a company that's as entrepreneurial as yours in the same market as yours. If none is available, wait six months. Repeat the process.

- Implement a sabbatical program for employees.

ALIGN COMPENSATION AND REWARDS

Many companies link compensation to performance, believing that it will motivate people to be innovative and make the company more successful. And on some level it may—at least for a time. However, to release creative flow, the focus needs to be on the success of the organization, not on the success of one individual or a select group of individuals. Here's a way to think about aligning compensation to help spark innovation and build a leadership culture.

First calculate the Total Maximum Compensation (TMC) that a person should receive. Some forward-thinking companies, such as Google, limit the amount of compensation for their highest-paid executives to a certain multiple of the lowest paid (e.g., ten times). Thus if $50,000 is the lowest, then the maximum that an executive could be paid would be $500,000.

I believe that corporate executives should be paid one half of their TMC in guaranteed, base compensation. So if the TMC for a particular leader is $1 million, then the base could be as high as $500,000. The remainder should be tied to the company's overall results.

Here are some forms of forward-thinking compensation you can use to reward people for performance, without putting a damper on creative flow:

Gain sharing: This is an awards fund that is based on how well the company does in meeting its goals. Every employee, regardless of position, receives a bonus in the form of a cash payment. These bonuses should be based on a well-understood process or formula—so that there is transparency and trust in the process.

Team recognition awards: By rewarding teams that do a superb job exemplifying the company's core values or achieving a specific goal, you motivate everyone. These types of programs typically include peer nomination and review—and the public recognition of the winners at an awards ceremony. My recommendation is to make sure no team consistently wins the award; the wealth and glory should be shared over time.

• • •

CONCLUSION

Companies that place a premium on building trust and generating spark will outperform all others. To spark innovation, you need to encourage people to put their full creative energies to work. Innovation doesn't flow from a business plan or out of a series of mergers and acquisitions. Innovation arises out of a deep appreciation of the importance of creative flow. Leaders should focus on discovering what people are good at, empower them to experiment, and praise them for their work. In leadership culture, there's no room for micromanagement. It's the leader's job to make sure the ingredients of creative flow are in place—and then step out of the way.

SPREAD SYSTEMS THINKING

$$(ACV + STF + LTO + MDW + SWY) + (APC + SCF + SST + MTC + APQ) = LC$$

Schoolhouse Software is the maker of software applications for school districts. During 2002–2003, when school budgets were hit hard by the economic downturn, CEO Bob Levine watched in dismay as his competitors undercut his product by offering a lower price with stripped-down features. "Our sales pitch was always about value," recounts Bob. "But our customers were starting to view our product as a commodity."

The problem grew worse when one of Bob's key salespeople defected to a competitor and began selling the competitor's product as the simplest, easiest to use, and most affordable. Several of Bob's major customers switched to the competitor. Bob grew very concerned.

In the face of these signals that the market was changing, Bob was reluctant to change his business model. He wondered whether it was possible to "de-commoditize" his product; all the while his sales numbers continued to erode. When Bob raised this issue with our firm, we urged him to use a systems thinking approach to solve his dilemma. We urged him to peel back his own assumptions and look hard at the market trends driving his business. We asked him to think carefully about how his business generated value for customers today and in the future—not in the past. He did. And he came to the following conclusions:

1. The market was indeed becoming commoditized.

2. Schoolhouse needed to match its competitors' prices in order to retain its installed base of customers.

3. Bob needed to change his narrative—the story he was telling his customers.

As a result of going through this exercise, Bob's management team developed new user groups. Schoolhouse focused on selling a "base version" of their software with added-value features that could be "turned on" for additional monthly fees. As Bob's management team took this vision to their customers, the response was exciting. "When we got out of our funk, we realized that what we'd been selling was not what our customers wanted," Bob said. "Our own internal thinking had to change. Once it did, we got back on track."

PRACTICE #8:
SPREAD SYSTEMS THINKING

....

To achieve a leadership culture, the power of systems thinking needs to spread throughout the organization. It's not sufficient if just a few people understand how your organization creates value. Everyone should be able to see it as a system of work that results in value to a set of customers. Everyone should be able to think in terms of building systems that result in the greatest value at the least cost. Thinking in terms of systems gives people the ability to make change occur where it is most needed. By spreading the power of systems thinking, people can become data-driven in their thinking, visualize their work from the customer's frame of reference, and adjust business processes based on customers' expectations, not internal assumptions or traditions. By spreading the power of systems thinking, leaders can instill deeper levels of innovation and performance throughout the organization.

THE TOOLS OF SYSTEMS THINKING

When you use systems thinking, you start to view everything that happens in your organization as a system. There are production and delivery systems. There are systems that generate the greatest value to your customers—and systems that create the greatest profit for the company.

There are market systems acting upon your organization. When you view things from a systems perspective, you develop a visual picture in your mind of the entire enterprise. When solving problems, symptoms become relegated to the background as you identify underlying causes. Small signals may become more important as you try to detect what's really going on. You see patterns of recurring behavior reinforced by either positive "learning loops" or negative "ignorance loops." You come to understand the importance of constantly challenging assumptions. And you appreciate that one can neither be too hasty nor too slow. Timing is everything.

Systems thinking teaches us to appreciate how a decision made in isolation can negatively affect others. It teaches us to invest in assuring that everyone can view the organization at a holistic level—and make decisions that take into consideration the implications across the system. One of our clients, a health-care company, continually battled this problem. For example, the medical information team made decisions about what was required for electronic health records without considering the impact on physician scheduling and patient flow. Doctors became infuriated by the additional time required. Patient complaints increased. We gathered everyone together, looked at the data, drew a visual map of the current system and its ill effects, and facilitated a series of decisions to improve the process. As a result, the system improved.

Systems thinking teaches us to see change and trends across appropriate time scales. Sometimes we underestimate the pace of change; other times we overestimate it. "A leader must be able to see the strategic importance of a particular trend, highlight it, and then instigate a response with the appropriate level of urgency" is how one senior manager puts it.

For example, when Intel's orders declined in the early 2000s, the entire computer industry went through a spasm of contraction under the assumption that as Intel goes, so go all the rest. This contraction resulted from an oversimplified understanding of the complex supply chain relationships within the industry. The assumption caused many chip manufacturers to be late responding to the boom that began in 2003.

Similarly, during the recession of 2008–2009, many people assumed that all industries would be affected. This assumption drove down the share values of virtually every company in every sector. But the downturn didn't affect certain industries—like technology and health care—nearly as much as it affected others, like financial services, housing, and the auto industry.

Systems thinking can help you appreciate the multiple ways that one can "frame" a problem. In the field of cognitive science, it's well understood that frames influence how people think about a particular issue or problem. Each frame typically oversimplifies the problem and inhibits systems thinking.

In the world of business there are many frames, depending upon where you're sitting and the view before you. There's the organized labor frame. ("The unions will take advantage of this.") Or the shareholder frame. ("Our profits are more important to our shareholders than protecting the health of the environment.")

We teach our clients to see their organizations holistically, asking them to look at it from five system perspectives—strategy, governance, performance, process, and people:

- **Strategy:** From this system perspective, you focus on the long-term market trends affecting your business. You think about your competitive position, where growth will occur, and what broad initiatives are required to capitalize on those trends. You respond positively by thinking about the long-term use of your resources and how to focus to achieve your most important priorities. You respond negatively by focusing too much on what your competitors are doing.

- **Governance:** From this perspective, you focus on the system of decision making that controls the direction of your company. You think about the relationship between your board of directors, your chief executive, and your leadership team, and what authority is designated to each. You respond positively by thinking about governance and being very specific about delegations of authority. You make sure people are clear about their respective decision-making roles. You respond negatively by blaming people for making misguided decisions when the system isn't clear.

- **Performance:** From this perspective, you focus on the systems for measuring performance—first at the overall organizational level, then at the level of the various business units within the organization, and finally at the team and individual level. You respond positively by deciding what metrics and targets to track at each level, and what systems of communication will best align business units and teams of people in understanding where they are succeeding—and where they need to improve. You respond negatively by paying too much attention to individual cases of poor performance.

- **Process:** From this perspective, you focus internally on the processes of producing value. You look at how sales are generated or how orders are fulfilled or how products are received or delivered. You look at measures of effectiveness and efficiency. You respond positively by thinking about how to improve cycle time, quality, and the IT systems that support the process. You respond negatively by singling out specific individuals for not managing a process consistently or efficiently.

- **People:** From this perspective, you focus on your system of hiring and rewarding people. You focus on how to get the right people on board and how to develop them in their roles. You look at the competencies you need and how you can develop people to their best potential. You respond positively by developing feedback systems that enable people to learn continuously, to receive coaching and feedback, and to take responsibility for their performance. You respond positively by rewarding people for excellence and performance. You respond negatively by selecting and promoting people based on arbitrary factors, such as how much you like them personally and how much they support you.

If you're attentive to these five perspectives, you'll gain a much richer appreciation of your organization—an appreciation you can share with others. The art of systems thinking is to make sense of it all by organizing your thinking and realizing that each perspective needs to be weighed against the others. Failure to do so can lead to errors in judgment.

For example, the benefit of the strategic perspective is that it enables you to take the long view and identify changes you have to undergo in order to achieve an important goal. Bob Levine used the strategic perspective to reconceive his business. But the strategic frame may cause you to overestimate the power of markets and overlook the value of internal innovation. American automakers have consistently made this mistake, lagging behind European manufacturers in developing trendsetting features.

In the process perspective, people can become so focused on reducing cycle time or improving efficiency that they forget to focus on what customers actually want. This is the problem faced, for example, by the fast-food industry. McDonald's became very efficient in delivering Big Macs and Quarter Pounders; all the while its relative share of the market continually declined.

In the people perspective, too much focus can be placed on one person at the expense of the organization. In 1995, when Michael Eisner, the CEO of Disney, hired Michael Ovitz as president, he thought he was getting someone who could be a successful number two. Much to Eisner's surprise, none of Eisner's lieutenants wanted to work with Ovitz. Eisner's shortsighted decision cost Disney hundreds of millions of dollars.

In the performance perspective, people overly focus on performance without looking at other circumstances. Capital One, for example, changed the terms on its credit cards without adequately notifying consumers during the financial meltdown of 2008. It then jacked up the interest rates on those same consumers to unconscionably high levels, losing its most creditworthy customers. By putting numbers ahead of relationships, Capital One managed to dig its way deeper into financial crisis.

Each of these is an example of shortsighted thinking, where the snapshot of the situation is overly simplified, and a more nuanced understanding would lead to more judicious decisions. Where effective systems thinking prevails, people learn how to step back and look at a situation from multiple perspectives, choosing the right course based on a deeper understanding of what's going on.

LESSONS FROM THE TITANIC

Here are more examples that may help you see the benefits of systems thinking. When the *Titanic* set sail from England in April 1912, the engineers who designed the watertight bulkheads assumed that the hull would never be breached across multiple compartments below the waterline. This led to the popular illusion that the *Titanic* was unsinkable. Thus, for its maiden voyage, the ship carried only enough lifeboats to handle a small emergency evacuation.

In addition, weather reports at the time indicated the weather was better to the north and that there was no danger from icebergs. So the captain sailed a more northerly course to avoid inclement weather to the south. The owners of the *Titanic* wanted the ship to make the crossing in record time, which motivated the captain to sail at high speed through what turned out to be an iceberg-riddled ocean.

The story of the *Titanic* illustrates two types of error in judgment. The first is *feedback delays*. The weather reports upon which the captain relied were based on anecdotal evidence from a ship that had sailed three weeks earlier. The second is *assumptions of causality*. It was assumed that water-tight doors caused the boat to be unsinkable. But in reality, the watertight doors couldn't handle certain scenarios—including the gash in the bow that caused water to invade several compartments simultaneously.

FEEDBACK DELAYS ON THE TITANIC

Feedback delays are all too common. It would be absurd to drive a car down a street and respond to a red light fifteen minutes after it occurred. Yet companies rely on two-year-old market research to determine whether their products or services are well positioned to meet consumer demands.

Assumptions of causality are also common. When videocassettes were introduced, it was assumed that the number of movie theaters would decline. Instead, home video viewing sparked an increase in overall demand for movies. There was a causal connection, but the underlying assumption was 180 degrees off.

When Disney made a huge investment in Go.com, it gambled that it could make a significant dent in the emerging Internet search market. But the Internet search business is a brutal marketplace—where consumers reward scale and where content providers are penalized if they give preference to their own content. Disney's brand could not drive audiences to its search engine and its investment turned sour. Consumers simply didn't behave the way Disney's executives assumed they would.

SYSTEMS OF WORK

No matter what your business does—transporting cargo, delivering better health care, protecting the environment—every organization produces things. But too often, people lose sight of what exactly it is that they produce—and thus they don't produce it very well. The key question that needs to be asked is: "What is it that you actually do?"[1]

When we asked how his organization helps children, for example, the CEO of one of our nonprofit clients said that they advocate for better laws. "Well, how do you do that?" we asked. He responded that they analyze pending legislation and recommend changes. "How do you do that?" They have smart lawyers and lobbyists who work with congressional staff. "How do you do that?" They keep a record of everyone who's voted on similar legislation and, based on their voting record, decide who is a swing vote and focus attention there.

So now we're getting somewhere. The next question is: "Who's the customer for that analysis?" And, "Are they completely satisfied?" It turns out the customer is a specific group of lobbyists who regularly visit members of Congress. "Are they happy with the nonprofit's analysis of members' voting records?" When asked, those customers told us that the analysis only looked at certain votes, so its predictive value was limited. More time spent looking at different votes would yield better information and a better likelihood of finding swing votes—and a more effective job at advocating for better laws.

We see this pattern particularly in public service agencies and non-profits: lost behind the important mission is an understanding of the specific work that needs to get done and who the customer is for that work. Getting to the bottom of that question is the work of systems thinking. As one CEO put it when his organization embarked on this exercise: "It may not be glamorous. But it improves results, so it's far better than what we've been doing up until now."

THE CIRCLE OF ASSUMPTIONS

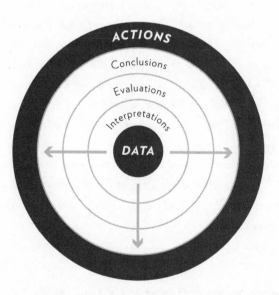

A helpful tool in helping people think about their assumptions is the Circle of Assumptions. As the diagram illustrates, when people offer their ideas about how to do something, there are rings of interpretation, evaluation,

(continued)

and conclusion around a central core of data. That core of data is too often hidden from view. To enhance systems thinking, it's important to share the actual data or observation, uncluttered and unfiltered by interpretation and conclusion. For example, in talking about the future of the U.S. auto industry, someone might say: "The U.S. auto industry is incapable of making a high-quality, fuel-efficient car at a profit. The industry simply isn't structured that way." In reaching that conclusion, this person relies on data: firsthand experience shopping for cars, tidbits picked up from the news, a chart in the *Wall Street Journal* showing the relative shares of the world market over the past decade.

But while those data are valid, they may not be sufficient to support the conclusion. Someone else may have different data, say the growth in the battery industry in the U.S. or the levels of investment in new fuel-efficient technology. That data may lead a second person to a different conclusion: "The U.S. is indeed capable of making fuel-efficient cars, and I'll bet that it owns more than 50 percent of the world market in ten years."

All right. We have a standoff. Both people have reached their conclusions. However, they have not shared with us the data that led to those conclusions. Nor have they shared how they interpreted or evaluated that data. Using the Circle of Assumptions, one could take a systems approach and begin to probe. "What was the data that led to that conclusion?" "Can you help me understand your reasoning?" Rather than trade opinions back and forth, the systems approach is to ask people to explain their reasoning and to trade in data. The Circle of Assumptions helps us visualize that inside every action and conclusion sits a closet full of assumptions, and digging through those assumptions leads to better understanding and ultimately to better decisions.

THE SUBSTITUTION FALLACY

When should a motion picture project move from editorial review to pre-production? When should a truck leave the loading dock? When should we shut down our production line for maintenance? These are typical business questions, and often they are answered in the same way: we assume that how we did it in the past is how we should do it in the future.

We call this the *substitution fallacy*. We assume we can substitute what we've always done for what is best. Or at another level, we assume we can substitute our own likes and dislikes for those of our customers. What's the right color for our packaging? We assume that if we like the packaging, it will sit well with our customers, too. We imagine that our wants, our desires, and our needs are the same as theirs.

But by using systems thinking, we can start to imagine that our customers' desires may be diametrically different. For example, when a large hospital in California decided to design a new patient intake process, its doctors, nurses, and hospital administrators had their own ideas about what people wanted when they first entered the hospital. Nurses assumed that patients wanted to get an initial assessment and then be taken to the emergency room in order of severity of their illness or injury. It never occurred to them that patients with less serious issues preferred to be treated outside the E.R. Administrators assumed that the E.R. should be a profit center for the hospital, and thus decreed that the costs of service should be higher than in the regular ward. Doctors assumed that patients didn't need to see them right away, when in fact patients rated an initial hello from the doctor as the most important part of the intake process. Each group fell prey to the substitution fallacy.

Conducting the research to understand what customers actually want is critical to overcoming the substitution fallacy. It means asking tough questions. What is the best process to treat each type of patient who comes to the E.R.? What criteria should be used to determine when the truck leaves the loading dock? When it's full? Or when the customer wants to receive the order? What's the best way to organize our inventory in the warehouse? By bar code? Or to maximize use of space?

Developing skill in asking the right questions is not easy. But it pays off. One of our clients invested in an internal group that specializes in training people how to apply systems thinking to improve business processes. This client—a large state agency—scrutinized its billing, auditing, and enrollment functions and weeded out millions of dollars in waste and inefficiency. They discovered that many of their processes were only partially connected to what customers wanted. Instead they were rooted in deep traditions and habit.

SYSTEMS THINKING AND ORGANIZATIONAL STRUCTURE

A large law firm in San Francisco faced the prospect of declining performance and increasing competition in its major practice areas. Our firm was asked to help.

Our situation analysis revealed that the firm lacked a consistent management philosophy. The major practice areas—intellectual property, real estate, probate, and corporate—each behaved like independent corporations. They had different compensation policies and different policies for managing employee workloads and billings. "You have four different cultures operating under the same roof," we told the managing partner.

From a systems perspective, this problem is known as *inconsistent management norms*. It can cause an organization to develop "bubble cultures" beneath the skin of the overall culture. Each partner within the firm managed according to his or her own ad hoc standards. Performance was inconsistent, which led to many conflicts within the organization. Their lack of a management system that could address and resolve these conflicts caused the partners to focus on their individual silos even more. People in the firm grew disenchanted with management, which then affected the firm's ability to attract and retain top-notch talent, which further fueled the decline in performance and propelled the cycle of management inconsistency.

Our firm facilitated a series of decisions that resulted in a new management structure. A three-person leadership team was empowered to set performance goals and standards across the firm. Once that team was in place, the culture began to shift. Norms were aligned to ensure the health of the whole. The bubbles disappeared. The conflicts that once paralyzed the firm were addressed because there was a forum in which to address them.

Many managers fail to address these kinds of structural problems because they perceive it as too difficult, or an admission of their failings as managers, or as overly taxing on people's freedom. In fact, the opposite is true. Tackling the issue head on, and developing a management structure that can integrate systems and create consistency throughout, is one of the best ways to reduce friction and build a high-performing organization.

Here's another example: When the founder of a large engineering firm decided to retire, it triggered a cycle of fear and paralysis among the three remaining partners. Rather than grappling with the gap in leadership, they each retreated deeper into their own silos. They asked our firm for help.

After interviewing the partners and other employees, we used systems thinking to help the partners identify the underlying problem. Because the retiring partner was the top producer for the firm, they had grown accustomed to doing the work that he brought in. Now the balance of rainmaking and project leadership was upset. The remaining principals had to decide whether to fully assume the rainmaking vacuum he'd left. Two of them chose to do so. One decided that his strength was in project leadership. This led to the creation of a new management structure with a CEO, a senior vice president of business development, and a senior vice president of client services. This new management structure, coupled with a two-year business plan, set the company on its feet again.

MORE STORIES OF SYSTEMS THINKING

Systems thinking means having the ability to view things in different time scales simultaneously and thus resolving the paradoxes between them. For example, our firm was asked to facilitate the transformation of a blighted urban neighborhood near San Francisco. We invited a number of "experts" to offer their views to a panel of residents. A city planner looking at the neighborhood told them that crime could be reduced by building new housing units. A group of residents argued strenuously that the key to saving the neighborhood was reducing drug dealing in the park. A cop testified that reducing crime would require a yearlong undercover surveillance effort.

When we introduced them to systems thinking, everyone agreed that the ability to transform the neighborhood depended on attracting new

SYMPTOMS VS. SYSTEMS

....

When you encourage people to use systems thinking, you're asking them to explore and identify the underlying forces at work rather than focus on the superficial symptoms. The table below shows some examples of systems thinking "lenses" through which you can view your organization and its environment.

SYSTEMS THINKING LENSES

LENS	WHAT YOU SEE	
	"SYSTEMS" PERSPECTIVE	"SYMPTOMS" PERSPECTIVE
Customers	Shifts begin in specific segments	New, old, desirable, expendable
Competition	Shifts in market positioning and branding	Size, proximity, growth, threat, opportunity
Technology	Shifts in technology driving new business models	What's working, what's broken, what do we need
Operations	Performance measures that integrate and align (e.g., balanced scorecards)	Different processes, work units, people
Management	Leading through purpose, core values, vision	Managing by objective
Partners	Synergies (or non-synergies)	Desirable, expendable

Most people become accustomed to focusing their attention in just a few places—on the competition, for example, or on technology. When you use systems thinking, you take a more holistic view. Using a systems perspective you also discover there are fewer variables to juggle. As you step back and view things from a longer time scale, you find it easier to pick out the critical issues to deal with. The result is a more balanced perspective, clearer thinking, and stronger leadership.

residents. They also agreed that the best way to do that was for the neighborhood to develop a deeper sense of its own identity and ownership. From these insights, a new neighborhood association was born, with 80 percent of residents taking part in regular meetings. A revitalized neighborhood watch group sprung up. Within a year, developers started constructing new housing units. Crime went down. People began returning to the neighborhood, buying properties. Neighbors celebrated their success with a huge street fair. The mayor hailed it as a model of downtown renewal. It made headlines in the daily newspaper.

These are the kinds of results that emerge from systems thinking.

When Darwin Smith first took over at Kimberly-Clark, he found a company thoroughly convinced that its future lay in the paper manufacturing business. Its culture framed its thinking in terms of production quotas and downtimes. He credits the tough conversations he had with his executive team, and the insights they reached together, for leading them to a different framing of their future—to exit the manufacturing business and excel in the products business. Kleenex and Huggies were the outcome of that vision.

HSBC Bank's global operations are guided by systems thinkers like Iain Stewart, who can integrate the immediate priority, such as resolving back-office processing problems, with the long-term vision to become "the world's local bank." Says one of his senior managers, "Iain's blessed with a toughness and an ability to analyze problems that few leaders I've worked with possess. He doesn't stop at the first or second level of analysis. He pushes to the third level—where everything is integrated."

MENTAL MODELS

One of the most powerful ways to grasp the importance of systems thinking is to remember that we all carry with us *mental models*. Mental models are the underlying habits that inform—and in many ways limit—our thinking.

For example, the CEO of a chemical manufacturing company came to us with a problem. The company was strapped for cash—and new equity investment seemed doubtful given the handful of customers they had. One of the opportunities for Bill's company lay in a strategic partnership with one of the top three automakers, which wanted to expand into the fuel cell–powered automobile market. Bill worried that a strategic partnership would "swamp our small company." He saw the company's independence being compromised.

The solution lay in examining Bill's mental model of the deal. In his mind, the strategic partnership would "swamp" his company. He would lose control. But Bill also knew the partnership would put his company on a more secure footing. With our help, the partners developed specific ground rules for how decisions would be made. For example, both sides would have to agree on any additional partners. Bill's mental model, which initially prevented him from seeing the deal positively, experienced a reframing. Talks progressed to the point where the two companies worked out a deal that was good for both sides.

Here's another example of a mental model. During the mid-1990s, Jim Thayer headed up the marketing department of a large international construction company. He was ambitious, smart, and good with numbers. Jim had a good sense of the market and knew his competitors' strengths and weaknesses. As a result, Jim was put in charge of developing new business opportunities around the world. Jim logged over one hundred thousand miles a year.

Jim managed up very well. He was always communicating with his boss and making him look good. Whatever the deal, Jim managed to make it work. He earned a reputation as a man who could make money "faster than bees make honey."

Jim was also pretty good at influencing his peers. He developed strong relationships with each of his peers on the management team. He made sure they got what they needed from his marketing department. He told his managers that internal clients were just as important as external clients. He developed a reputation as someone the other executives could trust.

Jim's weakness was managing down. While he enjoyed strong relationships with his boss and peers, Jim didn't develop good relationships with the people he managed. He didn't spend much time getting to know them. He didn't show much interest in coaching them or helping them learn new ways to tackle a problem. His mental model put himself first.

As a result, he developed a reputation as ambitious and self-serving. "I respect Jim," one of his managers said. "But I don't trust him."

When the company started looking at candidates for a new COO position, Jim thought he was a top contender. A consultant was hired to conduct an assessment of each candidate. The CEO was surprised to find that Jim rated low in the consultant's evaluation. "People just don't trust him," the consultant said. "People believe that Jim is out for Jim first."

An outsider was hired to be COO. The day after the announcement, Jim asked the CEO if he could get some executive coaching. The CEO said fine, he was open to that. Through the coaching process, Jim gained some insights into how his behavior affected other people. But he still didn't come to grips with his underlying mental model—his troublesome attitude toward subordinates.

Then Jim came home one day to learn that his eleven-year-old daughter had leukemia. Jim spent hours at the hospital to be with her. She nearly died. But after a year, she recovered. Jim said the process changed him forever. "After Lizzie's illness, I could never look at another person the same way."

Jim quit his job and opened a small investment firm. A close friend who watched Jim build his new company described it like this: "Jim was a changed man. He went from being a bulldog to being one of the most considerate people you'll ever meet."

People who work for Jim today describe him as trustworthy and open. "I know I'm going to get an honest opinion from him," is how one employee puts it. "He never uses hyperbole. When he gives me feedback, I know it's genuine."

Here's one more example of how systems thinking can help address underlying mental models. "I've got two vice presidents, both very good at what they do, who just can't get along," the executive director of a non-profit agency told us. "I spend an inordinate amount of time mediating their conflicts. What can I do?" she asked.

When we interviewed people, it became clear that the executive "mediated" these interpersonal conflicts by attempting to appease them. She told them what a fine job they were doing—and urged them to communicate better. She was learning the hard way the wisdom of Winston

Churchill's statement: "An appeaser is one who feeds a crocodile, hoping it will eat him last."

When we probed more deeply, it seemed clear that the executive was close personal friends with both of them. The answer became more visible to her once she donned the systems thinking goggles: One of her mental models was that she was afraid of what might happen to her friendships if she exercised her authority. Her other mental model was that shared leadership would mean that people shared responsibilities. Her blind spot was that her two friends were competing for her friendship. She had confused her personal relationships and her professional relationships—and so had they.

Using systems thinking, she came to grips with this fact. She realized that her professional relationships needed to come first. She explained to both vice presidents that she was no longer going to be able to socialize with them outside of work. She told them she would rely on data to assess how well each was doing. She then asked our firm to facilitate a process to put a new performance scorecard in place.

Using systems thinking, you can assess your blind spots and figure out your own mental models. What assumptions do you typically make that prevent you from making solid decisions about your company? If you look at yourself objectively, what could you improve? Think about the natural "cracks" within your organization. Where's the greatest tension? To what extent have you fallen victim to your own mental models? Are you making the appropriate investment in each area of your relationships? Are you communicating enough with your customers? Are you balancing the quest for new business with the retention of existing business? Do you meet regularly with your direct reports? Are you sufficiently focused on the financial data that can inform your decision making? Reflecting on questions like these will help you become a better systems thinker.

DYNAMIC COMPLEXITY

Peter Senge, the author of *The Fifth Discipline*, points out that human beings are experts at dealing with detail complexity but poorly equipped to deal with dynamic complexity. We are great at Cartesian thinking—dissecting a process or a machine into its constituent parts. But we are not wired to step outside ourselves and view a dynamic system of forces acting upon us and identify effective solutions.

It's our collective failure as human beings to grapple with dynamic complexity that results in the *tragedy of the commons.* Our brains are wired in such a way that we don't enjoy solving complex issues that would benefit multiple groups very easily. So we stay fixed on simple, linear problem solving to the detriment of addressing much weightier concerns.

The obvious example is the environment. We are dependent on the quality of our environment for the quality of our lives, and yet we seem unable to grapple effectively with global warming, declining water and air quality, and massive toxic cleanup. Systems thinking reveals the importance of these issues. Yet the tragedy of the commons continues. Why? In part because we are not equipped to grapple with dynamic complexity.

That poses a challenge for building high-performing organizations. The world is getting more complex, not simpler. To lead effectively means teaching people how to grapple with dynamic complexity. Here are some strategies for doing so:

- Create new sources of information to provide leading indicators about how your company or your industry is doing. Introduce new forums for sharing information. Bring new data and research to the forum and ask people to talk about the implications.

- Balance your teams to include a healthy mix of systems thinkers and linear thinkers.

- Ask people to shift their focus to understanding causes rather than treating symptoms.

- Hang up a diagram of the Circle of Assumptions, and ask people regularly to explain the data that led them to their conclusions.

- Root out distractions. Continually ask yourself: "What is the goal behind the goal? What do we want to achieve with this program? If we actually had this, what would it get us? How could we better invest our time, money, and people?"

- Create forums where people can share articles and books on systems thinking.

- Instill healthy competition framed around the core values and vision of the company. Form teams to tackle complex challenges, and reward the losers as well as the winners.
- Set up special "systems thinking" teams. Ask them to take a hard look at a particular process. Ask them to provide feedback and recommendations to fix any substitution fallacies, feedback delays, or assumptions of causality that might be introducing "noise" into the process.
- Teach people to minimize system delays: set standards for response times and decision making.

Once you start applying systems thinking to dynamic problems, you're more likely to find *leveraged solutions* that can result in quantum leaps in performance. For example, a major food supply company was having problems getting timely payments for the truckloads of food that departed its loading dock each morning. A team was formed to come up with a solution. After applying the rules of systems thinking, it occurred to members of the team to rethink the accounts receivable department. The accounts receivable people had always sat inside the Finance Department on the third floor. The team recommended moving the accounts receivable department to the loading dock.

The solution was brilliant. The AR people quickly taught the people on the loading dock not to load goods before they were paid for. The move resulted in a quantum leap in financial performance.

Leveraged solutions result in big improvements in performance. They come as a result of a clear vision of the outcome, innovative thinking, and breaking down mental models. They are critical for building an organization that can move at light speed.

• • •

CONCLUSION

Watching leaders and managers in action, I've observed that there are three major challenges to maintaining a systems perspective.

First, because we live in an era of accelerating change, it's easy to become distracted by the daily influx of events and issues—"to spend twenty-four hours a day fighting fires," as the vice president of a health-care system told me. Almost by nature, people tend to focus on fixing things: on the people who aren't performing, budgets that aren't met, or logistical issues that need attention. It's easy to become bogged down in the details and forget to use systems thinking to create leveraged solutions.

Second, people don't get training in systems thinking. Few companies offer it. Few human resource managers recognize its value. It simply isn't a priority. As a result, there is no forum, no conversation, for leaders and managers to engage in systems thinking together. Lacking a dialogue around systems thinking, it's easy to miss the opportunities and the benefits.

Third, aside from getting distracted by the day-to-day and the lack of training, it's human nature to avoid confronting deeply rooted problems. "There are some issues I'd just as soon leave alone," one manager said. "We have to pick our battles."

That may be human nature. But failing to listen to data, to challenge assumptions, or to use systems thinking to address underlying issues ultimately imperils the organization. One need look no further than General Motors, Lehman Brothers, or Enron. In contrast, think about Porsche, which has single-mindedly focused on engineering high-quality cars for twenty-five years. It's not an accident that Porsche is one of the most profitable automobile companies in the world. And, not surprisingly, managers at Porsche put a premium on core values, on disciplined performance, and on analyzing their customers and their competitors from a systems perspective. It's this kind of thinking that builds high-performing organizations.

MULTIPLY THE COMMUNICATION

(ACV+STF+LTO+MDW+SWY) + (APC+SCF+SST+MTC+APQ) = LC

At a daylong meeting with a group of neuroscientists at the University of California, I posed this question: "Aside from getting more grants to do research, what would most help you achieve a breakthrough in your field?"

"If we're to succeed," one of them said, "we need to understand what each of us is learning. Bridging the gaps is our biggest challenge—and our biggest opportunity."

"That's right," another chimed in. "We are so specialized in our individual research. It's like the big bang. Our stars keep flying farther apart from each other. It's almost like we can't see each other."

"We win our grants and build our reputations by specializing," said another. "Yet as we become increasingly specialized, ironically the biggest breakthroughs are when we collaborate between specialties."

I asked them: Has anyone tried to stimulate this kind of collaboration directly? "We put together an interdisciplinary team," one person said. "We met twice each week. It was slow going at first. But it yielded a brand new level of understanding about neurodevelopmental disorders."

Another scientist added: "We achieved a breakthrough in autism research when we built a shared understanding of what happens at three levels—behavior, development, and biology. Each specialty has a different history, different scientific protocols, and different language. It was a huge leap."

PRACTICE #9:
MULTIPLY THE COMMUNICATION

....

To build trust and generate spark, you need to multiply the patterns of communication throughout the organization. Internally, this means a focus on creating forums throughout your company where people can talk, share information, and continuously learn. It also means focusing on external communication. Since there is no "under the radar" anymore, leaders need to invent new ways to communicate and shape the rules of the game with customers, shareholders, and others.

This conversation about transcending differences and finding common ground to achieve a breakthrough was not new to me. But it was new for this group. I asked them what needed to happen for them to bridge the gaps more frequently.

"We need to rethink how we communicate," one of them said.

"So who is responsible for that here?" I asked.

"Good question," another scientist said. There was a pause. "I guess we all are."

People started to toss out ideas. They became energized. Within an hour, they had identified five new strategies to build new forums of collaboration and communication—and agreed to try all of them. They also decided to meet each quarter to assess how well they were communicating. They were making the leap to communicating in new dimensions. They were communicating about communicating.

THE IMPORTANCE OF COMMUNICATION

If these first seven chapters could be summed up in a phrase, it would be that they are all about new systems of communication. Take a look at the list of practices and the related changes in communication.

PRACTICE	CHANGES IN COMMUNICATION
TRUST	
1. Align the Core Values	• People regularly convene to talk about the core values—what they mean and how they are made operational. • Performance related to the core values is communicated and shared throughout the organization.
2. Sharpen the Focus	• Leaders and managers regularly discuss the organization's vision—and sharpen the focus around specific priorities to achieve it. • People regularly talk about progress made (and any barriers) toward achieving the vision and priorities. • Business units regularly talk about their priorities and align their priorities with the strategic focus.
3. Lead Through Others	• Decision-making roles are clarified. • Authority is delegated. • Expectations for teams and individuals are communicated regularly. • Team operating principles are discussed and communicated. • Meetings occur in the context of ground rules for productive communication. • People communicate about conflicts directly (without triangulation). • People regularly give and receive positive feedback. • People receive regular coaching and development.
4. Manage Decisions Well	• Delegations are clearly defined. • People clearly communicate whether a decision will be consultative or consensus based. • People regularly communicate about and clarify decision processes. • People regularly communicate about specific decision roles and responsibilities.
5. Start With Yourself	• People are able to regulate and control their attention and intention while communicating. • People master the four powers of communication.

(continued)

PRACTICE	CHANGES IN COMMUNICATION
SPARK	
6. Accelerate the Pace of Change	• Performance information is shared throughout the organization. • Groups regularly convene to discuss ways to improve performance. • Learning loops are created and communicated. • Groups regularly convene to talk about how to improve the learning loops.
7. Stimulate Creative Flow	• People freely express their ideas for improvement. • People explore and share new ways of doing things. • Management regularly encourages and celebrates innovations. • Managers regularly communicate 1:1 with employees about what they want to be doing.
8. Spread Systems Thinking	• Teams communicate about problems using a systems thinking approach. • People regularly talk about systems of work. • People regularly challenge each other to explain their reasoning and conclusions. • Systems thinking solutions and successes are regularly communicated and celebrated.

As I mentioned in Chapter 5, the word communicate means "to make common." To build trust and spark innovation, you need to use all the communication tools that you can. If you think you're already doing enough communicating, think again. You're just beginning. You're still in the three-dimensional world. You need to expand your thinking.

Let's look inside the organization first. There are at least four dimensions to consider—communicating up, communicating down, communicating across the organization, and communicating consistently over time. I call this communicating in "4-D." Every leader and manager I've met has a problem communicating in at least one of these four dimensions. Some are better with peers, others are better with their bosses, others are better with subordinates. Many leaders communicate well in three dimensions, but fail to communicate consistently over time. It's important to take stock of your weakest dimension, recognize what you need to do differently, and train yourself to compensate accordingly.

I coached the leader of an investment bank who was extraordinarily gifted at communicating with subordinates but terrible at communicating with his boss. John never let his boss know what was going on. Trust had eroded to the point that his boss was considering firing him. We initiated a weekly thirty-minute meeting with his boss in which John spent the first fifteen minutes reviewing key decisions he'd made in the past week and the second fifteen minutes focused on key decisions coming up. Over time, they rebuilt trust.

Most managers and leaders should double or triple the amount of time they spend communicating. Sure, it takes energy and commitment. But if you want to build trust and generate spark, you have to create an environment where people know what's going on, frequently share ideas, and build the habit of addressing key business issues without fear of retribution. It starts with you. Saying that you want more communication without changing your habits is silly. Ask yourself: "In an ideal world, how would I communicate more effectively?" "What information do I need to share?" "What regular forums do I need to create?" "How could I energize the flow of information throughout the company?" The best leaders create a variety of forums, including one-on-one meetings, department meetings, topic-specific forums, "all-hands" meetings, all-day retreats, and social gatherings.

When you talk to movie and stage actors, you learn that the best directors create a safe place where new ideas can be tested and communication and respect can grow. The same is true inside an organization. If it's not safe for people to talk, it's impossible for trust or spark to grow. The key is to triple or quadruple the level of communication. It may seem like an expensive investment. But as people begin to communicate in new ways, you'll feel the culture changing.

COMMUNICATING EXTERNALLY

Four dimensions may seem like enough. But leaders have to communicate with external stakeholders as well. When you include all the different external groups, the number of dimensions swells to *twelve*. Here's a checklist of external groups you need to keep on your radar—along with the important messages they need to hear:

1. **Customers:** Your customers need to understand what your company stands for. Is it low prices? Is it commitment to excellence? Is it speed of delivery? Is it all of these? Your potential customers need to know the same things.

2. **Shareholders:** Your shareholders need to hear how the company is doing—and where it's going. Obviously they need financial information. But they also need to hear your high-level strategic vision and plan.

3. **Suppliers and distributors:** Your suppliers and distributors are part of your value chain. Communicate with them as you would your employees.

4. **Regulators:** Many companies have regulators working next to employees. You should build trust with them by keeping them in the loop, just as you would your employees.

5. **The media:** The best companies aren't waiting to respond. They have an active strategy for cultivating reporters and getting their stories out.

6. **Watchdog groups:** Successful companies build trust with watchdog groups by actively engaging them in addressing areas of concern. You'll gain more in this day of instantaneous information by addressing issues and investing in change than in clinging to the status quo.

7. **Unions:** Successful companies build productive relationships with their unions by meeting and communicating regularly with union leaders. You can build trust by recognizing that you share common interests and have reciprocal goals (financial success and job retention). You can generate spark by engaging union leadership in understanding where the company is going—and the important role that union workers can play.

8. **Community leaders:** In whatever cities and towns in which your company operates, you need to cultivate relationships with the elected officials and leaders in those communities. You share common goals; it's best if you develop those relationships before a problem occurs where you need their help.

I could write an entire book on engaging and communicating with external stakeholders. So let me hit a few high points. First, you don't need different messages for each group. You need a unified message that resonates with all of them. Second, you need to leverage different forms of media in order to reach these groups. (That's another reason for a single, unified message: there's no controlling which group hears your message through which medium.) Finally, many people in your organization need to be trusted and empowered to communicate with external stakeholders. Given the rise of so many different forms of communication, a tight command and control strategy just won't work anymore.

DEVELOPING YOUR MESSAGE BOX

A useful way of thinking about communication is the "message box." The box should contain one to three key messages that drive all your communication. If you've digested the earlier chapters in this book, then you know where to look first: at your core values and vision. Those speak to the impacts and outcomes you're trying to achieve and should be the heart of your message.

THE MESSAGE BOX

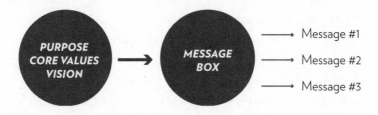

For example, your message box might be that "we are focused on only one thing: our customers." If someone asks how you're going to deal with financial setbacks, the first thing out of your mouth should be: "We are focused on our customers. As long as we do that well, we are convinced our financial situation will straighten itself out." Every communication begins with the message box. Staying in the box is hard work. It can feel repetitive. But the effort is worth it in terms of the consistency and trust building.

Remember that your message box should contain one to three simple messages. Don't try to customize your message to fit a specific group. If you have too many messages, people will hear different things, and they'll perceive you and your company as disingenuous. On the other hand, if you communicate from a place of purpose, people will sense the level of commitment and integrity. For example, your message box might be: "Our vision is to create long-term value for our customers, our shareholders, and the community. Our core values guide us in making all of our decisions." If you're asked why you want to build a new store or initiate a new partnership, that's your message. It can be that simple.

USING SYMBOLS TO REINFORCE YOUR MESSAGE BOX

Symbols are a powerful way to communicate your message. Symbols can evoke emotions, change minds, and impel people to action in a way that words alone cannot. Symbols can take many forms: they can be objects, actions, stories, rituals, or special language.

At EDO, a manufacturer of satellite equipment in Deer Park, New York, the lobby contains large illuminated models of the military satellites EDO has helped design and build over the past twenty-five years. The effect is powerful. Though no sign says it, the message is clear: "EDO is vital to our country's defense."

Symbolic actions can send an unmistakable message. When Dick Cooley took over at Wells Fargo, he ripped out the executive dining room and cut out other executive perks. The message was: "I'm serious about cost cutting and it begins with me." As mayor of Baltimore, William Donald Schaefer got fed up with the city's pothole problem and initiated an "Adopt a Pothole" program. Not only did it raise money for repairs, but it also generated national publicity and embarrassed the city's public works department into making pothole repair a priority.

Symbols play a huge role in successful advertising campaigns. Yahoo's name (and cowboy jingle) symbolized the irreverent, Wild West nature of its origins. For a time, Sprint's television ads showed a slow-motion pin dropping on a table. The message: Our service is so clear and quiet, you can hear a pin drop.

SYMBOL	MESSAGE IT REINFORCES
David Packard's humble home in Palo Alto.	Hewlett-Packard is about more than making money—it's about humility and teamwork.
Southwest Airlines' peanuts.	This is a different kind of airline.
Kimberly-Clark sells its paper mills.	We're no longer in the paper-manufacturing business; we're in the paper products business.
Elimination of private offices at Legg-Mason.	We're a team of equals—and we work together.
Louis Gerstner does away with the organizational chart at IBM.	We will no longer be fixated on ourselves, but on our customers.
Autographing of business cards when someone is promoted at Monster.com.	We celebrate each other's success.
"Associates" rather than "employees" at W. L. Gore.	We're all equally important.
Volkswagen television campaign: "Drivers wanted."	We're not selling you a car; we're asking you to join a revolution.

MOBILIZING THE MEDIA

In 2013, the most popular YouTube videos received 700 million views. In 2008, the most popular websites got two million hits. To put it in perspective, in 2000, when the dot-com bubble was bursting, you would have found slightly more than two hundred references online to "dot-com bubble." That's how explosively our media world has changed.

In a world where information moves so quickly, your organization needs to have a comprehensive media strategy in order to build trust with customers, shareholders, employees, suppliers, regulators, and all the other people who care about you and your organization. The first step is to ground your message box in your core values and vision. The next step is to mobilize the media and communicate in so many different forums that your messages are the ones that people hear.

What do I mean by "mobilize the media"? Every form of media can be your friend or foe, depending on how well you understand its versatility and potential, whether it's social media, traditional media, or something in between. Magazines and newspapers are investing as much energy and resources into social media as they are into traditional ink and paper. The lines between "new media" and "old media" are blurring. The lines may disappear altogether as all forms of media become more immediate, interactive, searchable, and customizable.

If media are used smartly, you can mobilize tens of thousands of people to your cause. The revolutionary change—the one thing to recognize—is that many of the new media are within your control. You no longer have to convince an editor or reporter that your message is interesting. You can reach millions of people directly. You can use social media to communicate with your employees; you can send regular e-newsletters to your customers; you can text message your shareholders when critical issues come before Congress; you can influence your industry by regularly blogging. In short, by actively mobilizing all different forms of media you can multiply the communication, lead the conversation, and communicate with different internal and external groups in ways that build trust and generate spark, all while bypassing traditional media channels.

WORKING WITH REPORTERS

At the same time, good journalism isn't dying; it's metamorphosing. Reporters are migrating from traditional print media to the digital domain—or finding ways to bridge the two. So while you can and should mobilize digital media to communicate directly, this doesn't mean you can ignore reporters and editors. They still play a key role—and should be part of your strategy for communicating effectively. So resist the temptation to view reporters as the enemy. Instead, work with them. Be proactive instead of protective.

What does it mean to "work with reporters"? It means to build relationships with a few key reporters who cover your industry, be available to them, and, in exchange, ask for their help when you need to communicate your message. Working with them boils down to doing four things well: (1) know what motivates reporters, (2) understand each medium, (3) establish good ground rules, and (4) build lasting relationships.

1. WHAT MOTIVATES REPORTERS

I used to be a newspaper reporter. I know from experience that reporters are not out to get you. First and foremost they're looking for facts or trends or interesting tidbits, the makings of a good story. Reporters like to get the story straight from the source, not from a spokesperson or public relations flak. So take the time to cultivate these relationships yourself.

Reporters don't like to be lied to or misled. Who does? But unlike mere mortals, reporters have the power of press. So if you're facing some bad news, face it squarely. Don't cover up. Tell them the truth the first time—and if you can't tell them everything, give them an honest explanation why not. "I can't reveal the details of our negotiations just yet because it could upset the talks at a very delicate point," is much better than "no comment." Lawyers will advise you not to talk to the media. I believe you should. It builds trust.

2. UNDERSTAND THE MEDIUM

Reporters have different deadlines and different needs, depending on what medium they work in. Television reporters have different deadlines than newspaper reporters. Bloggers need news right away. Magazine reporters have deadlines that can be as long as thirty to sixty days from publication. Understanding the unique needs of each medium takes practice. Ask them: "What's your deadline? What are you looking for? How can I help you?" You'll be amazed to discover that reporters respond favorably to acts of human thoughtfulness. Remember to always communicate your most important message first.

3. ESTABLISH GOOD GROUND RULES

Reporters operate on the basis of certain ground rules. You have a big advantage if you know what they are. The first rule is that any conversation with a reporter, no matter how casual, is "on the record" unless some other agreement is established *in advance*. Being on the record is only one of three possibilities. Your conversation could also be off the record, meaning it will not be used in any form, or on background, meaning it can be used, but without attribution to you. (In this case, you can define how the attribution will be characterized—for example, a "company official.")

Establishing the ground rules in advance enables you to control the discussion. Otherwise, you're at the mercy of the reporter. I coach people to say: "I'm happy to talk with you. But here are the ground rules I want to play by: Our initial conversation will be off the record. Once we've talked, you tell me what you'd like to put on the record and we'll discuss it." You would then ask the reporter whether he or she agrees to these rules. If the reporter agrees, the discussion would then proceed off the record.

Remember, you can control the game if you clarify the ground rules in advance. Some reporters may not like it—but they'll respect it. And if you hold fast to your terms, it's a deal they'll rarely turn down. (If the reporter does decline, then at least you know where you stand and can proceed accordingly.) Of course you can argue that this leaves you vulnerable to a dishonest reporter who goes against his word. But most reporters are honorable. Their reputations—and job security—depend on it.

4. BUILD LASTING RELATIONSHIPS

It's easy to find the reporters who cover your industry. Look for their bylines or their blogs. Cultivate them! Invite a reporter out to lunch or talk with them on the phone under the condition that the entire discussion is off the record. Talk about what expertise you have and the kinds of stories you could contribute to. Ask them what they're working on. If you treat reporters with respect, they are far more likely to help you over the long term. You won't get everything you want. But they will be far more likely to help you out.

Once you are in their database, expect a call. They may want background information to flesh out a story. Perhaps a quote. Don't hesitate to let the reporter know what you think might be a good lead to the story. A good relationship with a reporter can yield big dividends down the road.

Above all, think of a reporter as someone who has a job to do. If you can point a reporter to an interesting story, you will be considered a friend, someone who deserves a thorough hearing when the chips are down. So invest in the relationship, just as you would your relationship with key suppliers and customers.

ENGAGING STAKEHOLDERS

When a utility company plans a new transmission line, the law requires that property owners adjacent to the project be notified. When a developer wants to build new houses, part of the process is showing that you made a good faith effort to work with local neighbors and property owners to mitigate any negative impacts. In both of these cases—and many others like them—leaders have to learn how to engage stakeholders effectively.

When you engage with external stakeholders, the goal is to communicate your plans and solicit their input and make them feel part of the decision-making process. There are ways to do this that build trust—and ways that can destroy trust very quickly. Being clear up front about how the decision will be made is hugely important. Chapter 4 spelled out the different types of decisions and the value of decision maps. Capturing the feedback accurately is another key. Another key is that all relevant stakeholders be engaged, not just those friendly to your project. Last, it is best to create a forum in which people can hear one another's perspectives. That way, people can see that you are genuinely open to hearing a diverse array of feedback.

For example, when leading a California task force to develop new policies for health-care coverage, we assembled a diverse group representing insurance companies, hospitals, physicians, researchers, and consumers. Each meeting of the task force began with a review of the ground rules for decision making. Between meetings, we used surveys to assess the level of consensus around draft policies. Over time, as task force members saw each other's positions and learned to appreciate each other's perspectives, the trust grew—as did the number of agreements. By the end of the process, we had reached consensus on more than fifty recommendations to the legislature for policy enactment.

COMMUNICATING UNDER FIRE

Leaders should be prepared to deal with a crisis. It may never come, but you have a responsibility to be prepared.

When a crisis occurs, the feeling is like no other. Events unfold at a speed that is beyond your control. Small things are magnified beyond proportion. Confronted with a bewildering array of data, options, and demands, you're tempted to retreat into a protective shell, waiting things out, taking your cues from what other people do or tell you. Resist that temptation! When you're under fire, you should remember the twin dynamics of trust and empathy. Remember to protect other people first— customers, employees, and citizens. Not your shareholders or yourself. Protect the public and your customers, and the shareholders will follow. Why? Because the long-term reputation and goodwill of your organiza- tion are more important than any short-term risk to shareholder value or your own job security.

TRUST-EMPATHY MATRIX

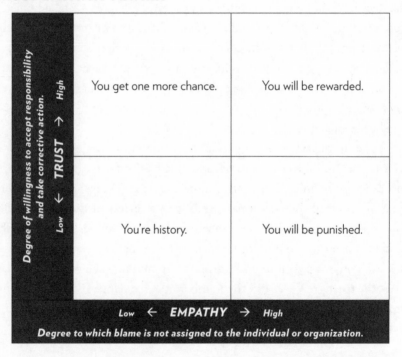

Take a look at the Trust-Empathy Matrix above. The Trust scale is within your control. How openly you respond under pressure will dictate whether you glide to safety or crash into the ground. If you communicate openly, communicate proactively, and provide all the facts as soon as you have them, you will build trust and the story will be less likely to spin out of control. On the other hand, if you withhold pertinent facts or leave reporters with further leads to uncover, you will erode trust. Reporters will attack people who mislead them. It is not pretty.

The Empathy scale is governed largely by circumstances. Someone or something caused a crisis to occur. If it is clear that you or your company is not responsible, empathy will go up. If you or your company are victims of some natural disaster, empathy will go way up. On the other hand, if you perpetrated a crime or accidentally caused harm, empathy will go down. Sometimes *way* down.

While the Empathy scale is largely beyond your control, there are things you can do to tilt it in your favor. Rule One is this: find ways to accept responsibility even if you're not at fault. This may feel counterintuitive, especially when someone else is clearly culpable. But reframing and expanding your level of responsibility will gain you empathy and help lead you out of the crisis.

A classic example is the Tylenol scare in 1986. When cyanide-laced containers of Tylenol were found on supermarket shelves, it was clear that a pathological killer was responsible. Johnson & Johnson executives could have focused on the criminal aspects and exhorted police to take responsibility for catching the perpetrator. Instead, the company recalled every Tylenol product, designed strong anti-tampering packaging, and conducted a massive awareness-building campaign. Johnson & Johnson executives understood the need to immediately take responsibility for the safety of their consumers. It is estimated to have cost the company $2 billion, but Johnson & Johnson emerged the stronger for it.

In contrast, consider another classic case. In 1989, the oil tanker Exxon Valdez went aground in Alaska's Prince William Sound. Eleven million gallons of oil spilled onto pristine shoreline. In the immediate aftermath, Exxon's CEO Lawrence Rawl was slow to accept responsibility. Instead he issued a flurry of press releases stating that the company was investigating the accident. The opportunity to contain the spill was squandered. Hundreds of miles of coastline were fouled.

Public furor built and the company's reputation plunged. Several weeks passed before Rawl grudgingly announced that the company would take responsibility for the cleanup. Eventually, thousands of workers and volunteers were mobilized to mop up the oil, save the wildlife, and minimize the damage to the extent possible. But Exxon's public image was left in tatters because its immediate response was too slow. William Reilly, then head of the Environmental Protection Agency, said Rawl's response was "a casebook example of how not to communicate to the public when your company messes up."[1]

THE LEADER AS HEAT SHIELD

When the organization comes under attack, its leaders need to become heat shields. They need to be the first ones to assume responsibility; they need to be the ones who accept blame and deflect it from everyone else. Here are five practices that help you be an effective heat shield.

First, maintain your perspective. Don't assume that people's first reactions are the right ones. Wait, gather data, and act when you have a good idea about what's going on. If a reporter calls, it's okay to say: "We're not sure what happened; I'll let you know as soon as we find out anything." Phil Jackson, the NBA basketball coach who had to handle some of the game's biggest egos, said he kept his cool by focusing on the big picture, by remembering that the whole season didn't ride on one game. Bad call by the referee? Jackson just stayed focused on the big picture. He was prepared to deal with the constant media pressure because he'd learned "to take his ego out."[2]

Second, use your sense of humor. The head of California's Public Utilities Commission, when facing hostile questions from the press about her role in the state's energy crisis, said: "Well, at least I didn't cause the polar ice caps to melt this year." Maintaining her sense of humor helped her appear cool, calm, and collected.

Third, be honorable. People respect honorable behavior—and nothing is more honorable than telling the truth and accepting responsibility. This requires more than words. In this age of media transparency, people need to see the proof.

Fourth, comfort people by validating their concerns. When it was announced that Merrill Lynch would be investigated by the Securities Exchange Commission, one Merrill manager assembled his employees and said: "We're feeling a lot of pressure right now, but I know we're going to come through it, together. I vow to keep you informed every step of the way." Because he validated their fears and provided them a way to vent their concerns, they felt safe.

Finally, have a routine that allows you to vent pressure away from work. Phil Jackson did it through meditation. Bill Clinton jogged and played golf. Every successful leader has some means to vent the heat and cool down away from work.

EARLY DETECTION SYSTEMS

The best way to avoid having to communicate under fire, of course, is to avoid the problem in the first place. Detecting a major problem before it happens seems difficult, but in fact the principles of early detection are well known to intelligence experts. It's what you do to *implement* such a system that matters. There are three key steps in the process: (1) decide what to measure, (2) build the system, and (3) establish an interdisciplinary monitoring team.

1. DECIDE WHAT TO MEASURE

You should be able to foresee what poses a significant threat to your business, your employees, customers, and key stakeholders: things like accidents on the job, embezzlement, workplace violence, faulty products, interruptions of service, and so forth. In deciding what to watch for, don't rely on lagging indicators like customer surveys. Look at leading indicators, like what your frontline people are telling you. One IT solutions company closely monitors how well its teams are doing in on-budget and on-time performance. They know when a team is off track and take action immediately. One of our clients developed a risk "heat map" that identifies seven categories of risk; for example, within the financial category, it lists credit rating, cash flow, and regulatory change. Red, amber, and green shading highlight the areas of potential concern.

2. BUILD EARLY WARNING SYSTEMS

Once you know what to watch for, the next step is to build monitoring systems. Utility companies invest in "fault detection systems" that search for evidence of line breaks and send signals back to a dispatch office. In large banks, the accuracy of transactions is measured by sophisticated neural networks. These artificial intelligence systems are constantly searching for irregularities, figuring that's where the gravest danger lies. The state of California uses complex algorithms to predict possible Medicaid fraud.

Early warning systems have to be tailored to your particular industry and needs. A retail grocery chain checks random packages for signs of spoilage and tampering. A business owner has the company's bank statements sent to her home instead of her work. "Even though I trust our accounting folks, they know I will be the first to spot any irregularities," she says.

When you build early detection systems, don't be tempted by the assumption that you can focus only on events that are likely to occur. It's the improbable event that will trigger the biggest problem. The key is to build forums of communication that enable people to talk about potential risks and determine whether adequate systems are in place to detect aberrations early on.

3. ESTABLISH A MONITORING TEAM

Once you know what you're measuring and how to measure it, people need to monitor and discuss the information regularly. It's a good idea to appoint an interdisciplinary team, including some people from the front lines. The team should be led by someone with a track record of staying cool under pressure and keeping an open mind. It should have the authority to raise red flags all the way to the CEO—bypassing middle management if necessary.

This team needs to be drilled to avoid jumping to conclusions. Under pressure, your first instinct is often dead wrong. It's too tightly wound up in past experience. For example, after the World Trade Center attack on September 11, 2001, the FBI investigated what it had known about the hijackers. Research turned up a memo written by an agent in Arizona that warned of Muslim extremists going to flight school. The memo warned of extremists piloting jetliners into buildings and that Osama bin Laden wanted to "finish the job" of bombing the World Trade Center. But higher-ups in the FBI were not notified because the information was not deemed sufficiently credible.

After the *Challenger* space shuttle blew up in January 1986, killing all seven astronauts on board, investigators went back to see what they could find. They discovered a string of internal memos warning about potential problems in the booster rocket O-rings. Management had ignored these memos. They had not deemed the evidence sufficiently convincing to justify spending hundreds of millions of dollars redesigning the booster rocket.

The bottom line is that any organization with a lot to lose needs to mitigate potential risks by establishing early warning systems and preparing potential responses. But all that planning is worthless unless people are trained in how to think clearly under pressure—and empowered to raise issues to the top.

• • •

CONCLUSION

To build trust and spark, you need to multiply the amount of time you spend communicating. Internally, this means sharing important decisions up, down, and across the organization, and consistently over time. Externally, it means communicating effectively with multiple stakeholder groups, including customers, shareholders, unions, regulators, and all the other groups you want to reach. If a crisis hits, remember the Trust and Empathy matrix. Don't duck and run for cover. Assume responsibility and communicate openly. And to avoid a crisis in the first place, create a multidisciplinary team to scrutinize the company for signs of trouble—and empower the team to raise a red flag if they see trouble on the horizon.

ASK POWERFUL QUESTIONS

*(ACV+STF+LTO+MDW+SWY) + (APC+SCF+SST+MTC+**APQ**) = LC*

In the last nine chapters I've talked about how to build a leadership culture. I've argued that the twin levers of trust and spark work together
to generate the highest levels of trust, productivity, and innovation. I've
argued that by focusing on these practices, you can create a culture where
everyone runs it like they own it.

In this chapter, I will talk about a tenth practice—one that will help
you translate these practices into your own organization. It focuses on one
of the most important tools of communication: the well-framed question.
This final chapter is where we talk about the language of listening and
how you can use these ideas to make a shift in how the people around you
operate as leaders. This final chapter is all about making these changes
real, starting with you.

Let's begin by talking about the process of personal change. It involves
three big steps:

1. Assume responsibility for the way things are and for making them
   better.

2. Become aware of your current behaviors and how they contribute to
   the current situation.

3. Commit to change, with specific steps to put into action.

These seemingly simple steps convey the essence of what you need to do to begin the process of change. Though seemingly simple, their power flows from the fact that they require you to explore yourself in ways that might lead to some surprising discoveries.

PRACTICE #10:
ASK POWERFUL QUESTIONS

Leaders need to assume personal responsibility for making change happen—both in themselves and in the people around them. Change means making a personal choice. Given that fact, leaders must learn how to communicate in new ways: rather than simply direct people, they must learn to ask powerful questions. "What is the change you want to make?" "How can you put these practices into action?" "What stands in your way?" "How will you measure your success?" By asking powerful questions, leaders can harness the power of self-reflection and help people assume full responsibility to build a leadership culture.

ASSUME RESPONSIBILITY

A man must be big enough to admit his mistakes, smart enough to profit from them, and strong enough to correct them.

—John Maxwell

To assume responsibility invariably means making a personal choice. This statement points to an important truth: no one can tell you to change. To change means making a choice. You have to choose to assume responsibility for the way things are. And you have to assume responsibility for making them better.

Assuming responsibility for making things better means confronting a paradox of the deepest kind: We cannot see what we want to become. We can only envision it, catch a glimpse of it, and even then only in our best moments. Assuming responsibility means asking a series of questions:

"What do I truly envision for myself? How do I want to be remembered? What is the legacy I want to leave? And how do I get there?" Developing your full potential as a leader means trusting in a different, better course—one that's invisible to you now. Remember: The word *leader* comes from a root word that means "to be out in front." The same root word also means "to die." You need to be prepared to shed parts of your old life to build a new one.

Once you start tackling these questions in a serious way, the door is open to all sorts of possibilities. You can identify your natural allies, your appropriate teachers, and the types of support you need to create. You can take the initial steps to change. Over time, you will come to see that highly effective leaders are continually scrutinizing their behaviors, accepting responsibility for them, and shedding parts of their old lives to build a better one.

JOHN'S STORY

John is a senior partner at a large L.A. law firm. When I first met John, it was after his partner called and said: "John's behavior is hurting morale in our office. Some of our most talented associates are leaving. He's dismissive of our younger partners. Could you talk to him? He definitely needs some coaching."

I set up an appointment with John for the following week. During our initial meeting, I recounted what the partner said and asked John whether he saw any need for coaching. "Do you see value in exploring what you could be doing better?"

"I'm one of the senior partners in this firm," he told me. "I've earned the right to do what I please."

I explained to him that the best leaders have coaches, just like the best athletes have coaches. "When you stop and think about it, everyone can improve in some way—no matter how advanced they are in their game or in their career."

Without comment, he asked me to explain the coaching process to him. I told him it would require a minimum three-month investment from him. John told me he thought it would likely be a waste of time.

"But if there are things I can do better, I'm open to hearing about them," he said.

I told John that in order to help him, I would need to conduct a 360 assessment. I asked him whose input would be most valuable. He gave me seven names: two partners, three associates on his team, and two associates whom he'd worked with before they moved to a different area of the firm.

"Please let them know I'll be calling," I said. "Tell them that this is a highly confidential process. I will summarize their feedback, but I won't quote anything they say directly to you."

In my interviews, I learned that people viewed John as a very talented lawyer, and as an excellent marketer for the firm. But people also felt John was failing to live up to his potential. Many of them thought John played favorites, often choosing the same people to be on his cases. They said he was dismissive of other people's feelings. Most telling, they said, John had made it clear in numerous ways that his most important priority was John, not the firm. One example that people cited was that John never seemed willing to let other people take the lead on any of his matters. "With John, it's me-me-me," one person said.

I assembled this information into a report, keeping who said what confidential. Under strengths, I listed John's technical proficiency as a lawyer, his marketing skills, and his ability to manage his relationships with clients very well.

Under the category of "areas to improve," I listed one: "Be a more effective steward of the firm. Put its interests ahead of your own."

I gave John this feedback. He listened attentively. He had a few questions. The main one was this: "Why should I change? I'm happy with the way things are."

He and I agreed to meet each week for several weeks. One day I observed him treat one of the younger attorneys in the firm abruptly over some trivial matter. When we were alone, I asked him: "Do you remember when your children first learned to crawl? They'd get stuck under the table, and then they'd bang their heads again and again trying to get free? And the more they banged, the more distressed they became, and the more they cried?"

"Yes," said John. Then he paused. "Are you saying I'm banging against the table? Because I'm the one who's trying to make things work better here."

"I'm suggesting you consider the deeper dynamics of this situation," I said. "When you 'help' people, they resent it. Why do you think that is?"

"I don't exactly know," John said. "Perhaps because I know more than they do."

"How do you feel when someone tells you what to do?"

John paused. "If I'm honest, I would say I don't like it very much."

"And yet you . . ."

"I tell them all the time what to do."

"I've also noticed that you come back feeling resentful, too," I said.

"They drain my time."

"What would happen if you really tried to help?"

John cast an eye at me. He came back a week later. "I have something to say," he said. "I took one of the junior associates out for a beer, someone I like, and asked her what she thought of me. She said I was arrogant beyond words. It caught me by surprise. I wasn't aware I was coming across that strong."

John paused. "When I became a lawyer, I was focused on what I wanted to do. I could see the city on the hill. I didn't really understand."

John's insight led to more uncomfortable truths. He realized he didn't communicate well with other people. He was quick to assert his own opinions because he was afraid of losing control. He was not adept at asking questions. He felt that he didn't fit well in a large firm. He needed to be in a much smaller, more entrepreneurial environment where he could be in charge. John left the firm a few months later. Metaphorically speaking, he died. But he died on terms of his own making, willing to face reality and commit himself to change. He opened up a small practice, specializing in intellectual property. A year later, John was a much happier man.

People at John's old firm were happier, too. With John's departure, younger partners had stepped up to assume responsibility for his clients. The managing partner reported the firm was no longer losing talented associates. In fact, two of them became partners a year later. From my perspective, this was a good outcome. John had assumed responsibility to make the change he needed to make.

BECOME AWARE OF YOUR BEHAVIORS

In studying the history of the human mind one is impressed again and again by the fact that the growth of the mind is the widening of the range of consciousness, and that each step forward has been a most painful and laborious achievement.

—Carl Jung

Once you accept responsibility for change, you need to become aware of your own behaviors and how you contribute to the current situation. This is not a job you can do yourself. You need people to help guide you. We live in an interdependent universe, and it's important to recognize your natural allies, the appropriate teachers, and what kinds of support you already have or need to create.

So assuming you've made a decision to assume responsibility for change, the next step is to find someone to be your mirror—your guide. Ideally, that person is a trained professional, a leadership coach. A good coach will help you in multiple ways, but three are essential: first, he or she will provide you perspective and raise your awareness about how you are perceived by others, both positively and negatively; second, he or she will be a sounding board, asking questions and offering counsel; third, he or she will help you pinpoint two to three behaviors to change—and help you instill new behaviors in their place.

An engagement with a professional coach typically begins with a period in which the coach observes. He or she will want to meet with you and ask questions. Often a coach will conduct confidential interviews to get a sense of what you do well and areas where you need to improve.

A coach might also use several assessment tools to help you build a more nuanced picture of yourself. There are personality assessments, such as the Minnesota Multiphasic Personality Inventory or the Myers-Briggs Type Indicator. The Birkman Method® can help you get a clearer sense of your natural preferences and needs. There are assessments of your communication style, such as Straight Talk®. All of these help you draw a picture of yourself in relationship to others. A coach isn't the same thing as a psychologist. A psychologist will help you understand how your past experiences influence your present behaviors. A coach focuses on your current behaviors—and your motivation for change.

Your coach may also want to trail you for a few days, observing you in meetings, watching you interact with your peers, sitting in on a meeting with your boss, all to help you get a keener perspective. Your coach may ask you to keep a journal or write a vision of where you've been and where you want to go. Your coach may want to collect 360-degree feedback. A good coach will be both a source of insight and a thorn in your side. If you don't get mad at your coach at least once, he or she probably isn't pushing you hard enough.

A coach should help you distinguish between *skills*, *competencies*, and *proficiencies*. A skill is something you master, like accounting. A competency, on the other hand, is open-ended and involves continuous learning. Marketing is a competency. Strategic planning is a competency. Finally, a proficiency is something you're naturally good at. Maybe you're proficient at building relationships. Or maybe you're proficient at figuring out computer algorithms. A good coach can help you identify your proficiencies and help you decide whether your professional role takes full advantage of them.

COMMIT TO CHANGE

Leadership truly develops from the inside out. If you can become the leader you ought to be on the inside, you will be able to become the leader you want to be on the outside. People will want to follow you.[1]

—John Maxwell

Once you become aware of your behaviors, the next step is committing to change. Your coach can help make sure this commitment is heartfelt and genuine. What is my vision for myself? How do I need to grow? What is my plan? This is the dialogue waiting to happen.

Using a systems perspective, a coach can help you see how several different problems might be caused by the same behavior. Through exercises and training, the coach can help you become more conscious of those behaviors, help you visualize the benefits of change. A good coach will help you recognize the behaviors that you need to change—and help you figure out specific new behaviors to implant in their place. Ultimately, your coach will want you to train your sights on one or two new behaviors that will help you become a more effective leader.

One of my favorite coaching lessons is this: "Act yourself into a way of behaving." If you can discipline yourself to try acting in a new way, very soon it will become ingrained. All that's required is the initial willingness to try.

When I think about this, I often remember the time I was living on a farm near Charlottesville, Virginia, with my wife and our two daughters. There was a mile-long gravel road to our house that followed a small stream before veering up the hill to our home.

One April, a huge storm dumped six inches of rain. As the rain pelted down, the stream filled quickly and expanded into a tumultuous torrent. The stream undercut the road and sliced away huge chunks of the hillside. In the pounding rain, I knew I had to save the road. But what could I do? I couldn't make it stop raining.

I had a flash of inspiration. In the driving rain, I took a shovel and began digging a shallow trench, starting at a point downstream safely away from our road, extending it to a point upstream where the stream was also safely clear of the road. I cut the trench just deep enough to coax a small trickle into it. Then I stood back and watched.

At first, the impact was negligible. But with a few whacks of the hoe, the water began flowing with more vigor. A few more blows released still more water into the cut. I watched in amazement as the trench filled with water. Within fifteen minutes, the old stream was gone, a new one in its place. The road was saved! And I had done it all by harnessing the stream's own power.

I tell this story because it illustrates to me an important principle of change. Start small. Figure out one behavior to practice. Ask people for feedback. And harness the power. Once you get positive feedback, the change will deepen. Soon enough, the new behavior will feel like the most natural thing in the world.

A coach can ask you to do things you wouldn't do yourself. He or she can focus your attention on a particular pattern of communicating or a style of managing people that stands between you and more effective leadership. A good coach can help you identify specific strategies that will make you more effective and capture them in a written plan of change. The goal is to help you cut a new course for yourself, to break yourself free of old habits and adopt new ones.

A good coach will help you act your way into a new set of behaviors. He or she will give you specific things to try, like communicating in a softer tone of voice when you are angry or preparing action items for each meeting in advance. At first, it will feel unnatural. With each step, your coach will be your sounding board, helping you reflect on what worked and what didn't work, helping you become the leader you want to become. With humility and conversation as your leverage points, you can start experiencing what it's like to manage and lead in a new way. Over time, as you stick with it, these new behaviors begin to feel hardwired. You will have shed your old way of behaving. You will have changed.

OTHER CATALYSTS OF CHANGE

There are other techniques and experiences that can catalyze personal change. Coaching and mentoring, which were discussed in Chapter 3, can be extraordinarily effective in moving you to the next level of leadership. In addition, here are three other approaches to consider.

PEER GROUPS

A peer group is typically a circle of colleagues from other companies that meets regularly to discuss professional challenges and celebrate successes. They typically bring diverse perspectives—a skeptic, an optimist, a futurist. In a typical forum, the group meets monthly and picks one or two timely issues to explore. If the group meets regularly, they will care enough about you to want to help—yet be sufficiently independent to offer good advice. When faced with a sticky issue, this is a group you can turn to and say: "I really need your help with this."

For example, when the founder of a venture capital company learned one of his key partners wanted to split away from the firm, his peer group provided valuable counsel. "More than anything, they kept me focused on what was important," he told me. "They advised me to get it over quickly so we could all move on. Despite my instinct to fight for every last nickel, I took their advice and we worked out a quick settlement that was more profitable for me in the long run."

ADVENTURE LEARNING

One avenue to personal growth and change is via adventure learning. By doing physically demanding things outside your normal comfort zone, you can go beyond your day-to-day coping mechanisms and discover what's truly important. Here's an example.

Several years ago I joined twenty other leaders in a redwood forest in the Sierra Nevada foothills near my home in Northern California. Strung high in the trees around us was a cobweb of woven rope lines, steel cables, and cargo nets. The instructor divided us into groups of two. I was paired with Ray, the leader of a nonprofit organization.

When it was our turn, Ray and I clipped belaying ropes to our climbing harnesses. We climbed up a seventy-five-foot rope ladder to a small wood platform high in the trees. In the distance we could see the sunlight sparkling off a blue lake. Down below, our instructor shouted words of encouragement. Stretching before us, attached to the small platform, were two thick cables. Where we were standing, the gap between the cables was about three feet. Farther out, the gap was ten feet. Our task was to venture onto these cables, Ray on one, me on the other. As we walked out, we would support each other by gripping each other's shoulders. Initially, the going would be easy. Eventually, however, the gap would become too great and we were going to fall. Our belayers would catch us when we did. But still—we were destined to fall. The only question was: When? How far could we support each other?

Here are the notes I took on the experience:

We're about three feet apart. Ray is facing me. We lock eyes and move slowly away from the platform. One step, then another, our feet sliding in a synchronous motion, our hands on each other's shoulders. We take a moment to enjoy the view of the redwood trees and the sparkling lake beyond.

"Looking good," our belay team shouts from down below.

"Tuck your butts in," someone shouts.

As we straighten our bodies, we feel more stable. Purely from an architectural point of view, we're trying to create a triangle. Our bodies are the two sides. An imaginary line between the two cables is the base (though an ever-expanding one— which is the problem!). So long as we are stable, the base is stable. So long as our belayers are there, we are confident in our ability to take one more step outside our comfort zone.

"What are you thinking about?" I ask Ray.

"Simplicity," he says.

I get what he means immediately. Every other worry has boiled away. We have a single purpose.

"One more step," I say. We are starting to sweat. I can feel the muscles in my arms burn. One more step and our bodies are close to a 90-degree angle, supported only by each other.

"This is good," I say. "Good and simple."

Ray grins. "Yep, we're fine so long as we relax."

We take a deep breath again, and then one more step. The pressure on my legs is growing. "I wonder if anyone's ever made it all the way across," I say.

"Only NBA players," Ray jokes.

I take one more step. The team below is cheering wildly. "You're almost horizontal," shouts one of the belayers. They urge us on. I try to lift my foot again and shake my head.

"I think we can make one more step," Ray says. "Let's do it in unison." We both try to lift our feet at the same time, but the motion nearly makes us fall. "Nope, that doesn't work," I say. "You go, and then I'll go."

I inch along, my shoulders growing numb. The belay rope tugs at my harness. Our heads are against each other and I'm looking right into his eyes.

"What do you think?" he says. "Ready to step off?"

"We could just stay here."

We laugh. Then we count out. One-two-three and step into the air. We fall toward the ground, there's a momentary sense of panic, and then a jerk, and a feeling of utter exhilaration as we float to the ground.

Later, when everyone's gone through the same exercise, we debrief each other on our experience. Everyone is smiling. "Fear is the great leveller," someone says.

"I wish I could feel this good every day," says another.

"What comparable challenges do we each face?" someone asks.

We look at each other.

"Up there, we have a choice," someone says. "We can either choose to stop going. Or we can take the next step into the unknown. And every member of this team chose to keep going into the unknown."

GROUP LEARNING

Another avenue for personal change is to take part in a group activity that pushes you to explore your emotional roots in a deeply personal way. This deeper emotional level is where real awareness building and change can occur. There are established groups, such as the Hudson Institute or the Landmark Forum, expressly designed to bring professional people together to provide insight into one another's lives and help them succeed professionally.

Here's how these kinds of experiences work: A group of fifteen to twenty people gathers for three days of intensive work. Then they return again for another five days of work. Over the course of these sessions, a trained counselor, usually a psychologist, leads the group through a series of exercises. People reflect on the important influences in their lives, both positive and negative. Through guided meditation, they are asked to reflect on early experiences of pain and loss. They are asked to identify how their parents affected them—and what inner "laws" they have been left with.

Understanding these inner laws gives us clues about our subconscious behavior. Do you see yourself as worthy of love, for example, or as always needing to please other people? Do you see yourself as incapable of greatness? Or as deserving success? Through a series of personal exercises, people are asked to confess to the group the deepest laws that govern their behavior.

At some point, the members of the group get a chance to provide feedback, again both positive and negative. Arrogance, timidity, and insincerity are frequent themes. People reflect on this feedback and try to let go of the inner fears that trigger them. After hours of reflection and meditation, people take a break and talk about what they've learned about themselves.

The next step is a rebirth. People are asked to identify the one inner law they wish to change. People symbolically enact a rebirth of themselves. It is a joyful experience. You are asked to write down your own charter of change, distilling what you've learned into new laws to incorporate into your life.

These types of group experiences leave you humbled, drained, and deeply reflective. One executive swore that it was the most important thing he'd ever done. At his urging, all of his executives also went through the experience. After a few months, the joy and jubilation of self-discovery wears off, but a deeper recognition remains: You can be a new person, with new rules guiding your behavior. Your worst fears are behind you. Your old laws can be replaced by new ones.

I don't want to mislead you into thinking that one weekend will necessarily turn around your life. But it can wake you up and provide profound insights. It can certainly help you understand what work needs to be done. And that kind of self-insight is an important step for anyone who aspires to be a leader.

BECOMING AN AGENT OF CHANGE

This chapter is not only about your personal change. It's about becoming a change agent within your own organization. Remember the axiom: assuming responsibility means making a choice. Given the truth of that statement, what can you do to help other people change their behaviors?

You can't *tell* them to change. You can't direct them to assume responsibility. If you want real change to occur, you need a different type of communication.

When John F. Kennedy said: "Ask not what your country can do for you—ask what you can do for your country," he was asking a powerful question. He was honoring the fact that people have the freedom to choose. His question was the ultimate question: "What could you do for your country?" His question was heartfelt, and it contained no preordained answer. But he was doing what all great leaders do: he was asking powerful questions.

To help people change, you need to ask powerful questions. Not your opinions or advice masquerading as questions, but powerful, open-ended questions that evoke genuine reflection. Asking powerful questions is not natural. It is not something we are trained to do. Our culture teaches us to express ourselves, to speak our opinions, to say what we feel, without stopping to ask powerful questions. Yet the fact is, the art of catalyzing change boils down to asking questions, listening carefully, and engaging people in deep reflection. It means asking enough of the right kinds of questions and listening with enough care so that people say: "I see now what I need to do. It's my responsibility to make this better."

We saw in Chapter 4 how people are naturally prone to thinking that everything they're doing is okay (it's everyone else who is screwing up!). Reflect for a moment on what this implies. If real change entails asking people powerful questions, how can you create the forums in which people can be self-reflective? How do you create the conditions for real listening to occur? How do you start asking powerful questions?

GLORIA'S STORY

Gloria remembers vividly her first week on the job working for a large bank. People were sullen. There was no sense of fun. Her first day on the job seemed interminable. Not a single person came up to say hi to her. She described it as "the worst day in my life and the worst work culture I'd ever seen."

On the third day, a voice intoned over the intercom that a birthday celebration was going to take place at four o'clock in the conference room.

"Great," said Gloria to herself, "a little human interaction." But when she arrived promptly at four o'clock, she found the conference room empty. A sheet cake listing five people's names—none of whom were there—sat on the table. Over the next thirty minutes, a few people straggled in, helped themselves to a piece of cake, and left. Only two of the birthday honorees bothered to attend. There was no singing, no festivity, and no conversation. No one stuck around.

By the end of the first month, Gloria was ready to quit. Naturally an open, optimistic person, she had begun to feel introverted and insecure. She avoided eye contact with her coworkers. To her friends, she confessed how deeply troubled she was by the organization. But at work she kept her thoughts to herself.

One day, however, she was asked by one of the partners in the firm to share her impressions of the firm. She decided to seize the moment. She recited to him a litany of problems: poor communication, low trust, people feeling underutilized and abused. She was scathing in her criticism of the managing partner, a former Army colonel. He ran the place like a boot camp.

Thinking no more of it, she left his office. The next day she was at a meeting when the colonel himself walked in. Before she could escape, the colonel said: "Gloria, I understand you have some feelings about the way I run things around here. Would you mind telling them to me, right now?"

Gloria blushed. "Since it appears my thoughts have already been shared, let me give them to you directly." Fully expecting to be fired, Gloria unloaded. After she was finished, the colonel pulled out his pocket calendar. Gloria was convinced he was ticking off the thirty-day notice he was about to give her.

Instead, he said: "Can we meet here again in fifteen days? I want you to tell me whether you see any changes."

Gloria was thunderstruck. But she accepted his offer. Over the next fifteen days, she did see some changes. She noticed that managers were more communicative. She noticed that the colonel solicited people's views more often. After fifteen days had passed, Gloria met with the colonel and told him she'd seen a few encouraging signs of change.

"But it's not enough," Gloria said. "People still don't trust each other. Do you really want the culture here to change?"

"Yes," he replied. "But I need help. Are you willing to sign on for the biggest challenge of your life?" He paused. "Would you help me transform this into a place where people love to work?"

Gloria thought about it. She wondered whether he was serious. But ultimately, she decided to take a chance. She told the colonel she would do it under two conditions: "I need your full, unconditional support for this work—and I need you to recognize it will take months and years, not days."

"Wonderful," he said. "You're in charge. You figure out what we need to do and I'll support you."

So over the next several months, Gloria enrolled hundreds of employees in the change process. She developed a strategic plan for the organization. She engaged everyone in powerful questions about their roles in implementing the plan. She created learning loops; she delegated authority; she nurtured people's creative flow. She even coached the colonel.

As the months passed, the colonel's communication patterns changed dramatically. He became more open to feedback. He asked more questions. He was more humble. He cracked jokes at his own expense. A sense of joviality and fun began to pervade the culture. Performance began to rise, too. Turnover decreased. Talented people elected to stay.

Over the years, Gloria and the colonel became very close—so close that they vowed to leave the bank at the same time—which they did, fourteen years later.

CREATE REAL, MEANINGFUL CHANGE

Chapter 6 focused on practices that enable your organization to keep pace with change. It stressed that in today's business environment, the pace of change is accelerating, and that it's a leader's job to use learning loops to help people embrace continuous, accelerating change. Now we're talking about helping people change their individual habits. We know that the key is asking powerful questions. But the question is: Who will ask those questions? Who starts the ball rolling? Where do we begin?

The answer, faithful reader, is that we begin with you. You're the one who now understands these practices. You are the one who now understands how to help people assume responsibility. The tenth and final practice is for you to create a new role for yourself in your organization. Combined with the other nine practices, this is the culmination of the leadership equation. This is how you start building a leadership culture.

For each of the ten practices, there are powerful questions you can ask. To help you get started, here are the ones that can have the most impact:

1. **Align the Core Values:** "What would happen if everyone in our company shared a deep understanding of our company's core values—and lived up to those core values every day? What if everyone participated regularly in discussing the meaning of our core values and how to better translate them into practice? What specifically might that do to improve our effectiveness as an organization? What conflicts might it resolve?"

2. **Sharpen the Focus:** "What would happen if our entire organization were united around a common vision? What would happen if we truly focused on achieving a few major priorities? What would that do for our performance? What conflicts would it resolve?"

3. **Lead Through Others:** "What if we focused on getting the right people into the right roles each and every time? What would happen if we had a consistent approach to teamwork—and what it means to be both a team leader and a team member? What if we had operating principles that helped people identify and address conflicts quickly? What if trust were pervasive and fear was unknown in our company? What would we have to do to achieve that kind of culture?"

4. **Manage Decisions Well:** "What would it be like if everyone in our company understood what decision-making authority was delegated to them? What if everyone in the company felt empowered to suggest ideas and suggest change? How would it be if we were crystal clear about how we were making a given decision? What would it be like if our board and our CEO were clear on their respective authorities?"

5. **Start With Yourself:** "What if every manager and leader in our company demonstrated humor and humility? What if everyone consistently behaved honorably and with heartfelt passion for what they do? What if everyone communicated with an affirming intention and acute awareness of different styles of communication? How would that change our culture?"

6. **Accelerate the Pace of Change:** "What would happen if we had performance metrics tied to every major business product and service we offer? What if the information related to those metrics was shared immediately with people at the front lines? What if we empowered people to suggest ideas for improvement—and accepted their ideas nine times out of ten? What if we embraced continuous improvement as part of our day-to-day work? How would that affect our performance?"

7. **Stimulate Creative Flow:** "What would happen if we tapped into people's creativity more often? What if we were more aware of the things that each person most enjoys doing? What would happen if people were free to collaborate across departments? What would happen if we created incentives for people to experiment and try things without anyone looking over their shoulders or prematurely judging them?"

8. **Spread Systems Thinking:** "How do we create value in our organization? What would happen if everyone in our organization understood those systems? What if everyone thought more about our business as a system and appreciated the full consequences of their decisions? What if everyone heard from their customers more frequently (both internal and external customers)? How might that affect our company's performance?"

9. **Multiply the Communication:** "What would happen if we had ten times the amount of communication up, down, and across our organization? What would it be like if information flowed quickly from those who have it to those who need it? What would happen if we communicated more regularly with our customers and other outside stakeholders? How would that affect our performance?"

10. **Ask Powerful Questions:** "What would it be like if everyone in the company assumed responsibility for asking powerful questions. What would happen if everyone then asked what it would take to make that happen, and how we would measure success? What would we have to do differently? How could we build that kind of culture?"

• • •

CONCLUSION

Effective leaders create a culture in which people strive to improve themselves. In this chapter, we learned that the journey of personal growth begins with three steps: (1) accepting responsibility, (2) becoming aware of your behaviors, and (3) committing to change. Because accepting responsibility involves making a personal choice, effective leaders focus on creating cultures in which people ask powerful questions of each other. Because it is difficult to become aware of your behaviors on your own, effective leaders encourage people to find coaches and mentors.

But being an agent of change also means understanding the dynamics of organizational change. Effective leaders use powerful questions to engage people and get them to assume responsibility for new ways of thinking, acting, and behaving. When a leader asks powerful questions and listens attentively, powerful ideas emerge. When hundreds of people from all different levels of the organization come together and talk seriously about the ways they want the company to improve, the energy and momentum can last for years. When everyone regularly engages in this kind of powerful listening, the result is the highest levels of trust and spark.

CONCLUSION

MAKING THE JUMP

Over the course of this book, I've described ten practices that build trust, generate spark, and create a leadership culture. As you've read about these practices, I hope you've thought about how you can use them to propel your organization to higher levels of performance. In so doing, here are five final powerful questions to consider:

1. Thinking back over this book, which practice would you most like to put into effect right away?

2. Why? What would you hope to accomplish?

3. What would you have to do, starting now, to make that happen? What would be your immediate next steps?

4. What obstacles might you encounter? How would you overcome them?

5. How would you measure your success six months from now?

If you've taken the time to answer those five questions, then you're already putting the leadership equation to work in your own organization.

Here are two other helpful tools. First, you can get a detailed look at how well you and your organization are doing in building trust and generating spark by taking our free assessment. You'll find the survey at our website: www.leadingresources.com. Click on The Leadership Equation icon on the home page. After answering a series of questions, you'll get a series of scores for each of the ten practices described in this book—along with a visual diagram of your organization's strengths and opportunities for improvement.

Second, I've written a number of detailed tools that will help you put these ideas to work. By subscribing to our newsletter, you'll get these tools for free. (You can subscribe at our website.)

Last, if you're serious about putting these practices to work in your company, our team is here to help. We can coach you through the process. We can assess where you are—and where you need to go. We can help make sure that you implement these practices in a phased, pragmatic way that delivers the greatest return on your investment while ensuring your organization's long-term sustainability—and that ultimately, helps you create your own leadership culture.

NOTES

Introduction

1   In my earlier book, *Straight Talk*, I described many of the specific techniques of communication that distinguish productive teams (*Straight Talk: Turning Communication Upside Down for Strategic Results*. Palo Alto, CA: Davies-Black, 1998.

2   Michael Kosfeld, Markus Heinrichs, Paul J. Zak, Urs Fischbacher, Ernst Fehr. "Oxytocin Increases Trust in Humans," *Nature*, June 2005.

3   Steven Pinker, *How the Mind Works* (New York: W.W. Norton & Company, 1999).

4   "How to Keep Your Company's Edge," *Business 2.0*, December 1, 2003.

5   "How to Create Cool Technology," *Business 2.0*, December 1, 2003.

6   Bob Thomas, *Walt Disney: An American Original* (Disney Editions, 1994).

7   David Osborne and Ted Gaebler, *Reinventing Government: How the Entrepreneurial Spirit Is Transforming the Public Sector* (New York: Penguin Books, 1992).

Build Trust
Practice #1: Align the Core Values

1   Jim Collins, *Good to Great: Why Some Companies Make the Leap…and Others Don't* (New York: HarperCollins, 2001).

2   Ibid.

3   John Byrne, "After Enron: The Ideal Corporation," *Business Week*, August 13, 2002.

4   Abraham Maslow's work on personal core values is highly important in understanding social dynamics and the sources of human conflict and fulfillment. See Abraham Maslow and Deborah Collins Stephens, *The Maslow Business Reader* (New York: John Wiley and Sons, 2000).

5   "Global Leadership and Organizational Behavior Effectiveness," May 2009, www.thunderbird.edu/wwwfiles/ms/globe.

6   John Rawls, *A Theory of Justice* (New York: Oxford University Press, 1999).

7   This chapter focuses on developing the framework of core values. Chapter 3 focuses on tying performance measures to the framework.

8   Procter & Gamble, "Our Values and Policies," Procter & Gamble website, April 2009, www.pg.com/images/company/who_we_are/pdf/values_and_policies907.pdf.

Practice #2: Sharpen the Focus

1 Steve Lohr, "He Loves to Win. At I.B.M., He Did," *New York Times*, March 10, 2002.

2 Larry Page and Sergey Brin, "'An Owner's Manual' for Google's Shareholders," May 2009, http://investor.google.com/corporate/2004/ipo-founders-letter.html.

3 Jennifer Basye Sander and Peter J. Sander, *Niche and Grow Rich: Practical Ways To Turn Your Ideas Into a Business,* (Entrepreneur Press, 2003).

Practice #3: Lead Through Others

1 Dizzy Gillespie, Jazz Quotations, http://www.danmillerjazz.com/jazzquotes.html.

2 Patrick Lencioni, *The Five Dysfunctions of a Team* (San Francisco: Jossey-Bass, 2002).

3 Robert Fulghum, *All I Really Need to Know I Learned in Kindergarten* (New York: Ballantine Books, 2003).

4 Source: Interviews and published company materials.

5 My earlier book *Straight Talk: Turning Communication Upside Down for Strategic Results* details various techniques for managing meetings effectively.

6 The Arbinger Institute, *Leadership and Self-Deception: Getting Out of the Box* (San Francisco: Berrett-Kohler Publishers, 2000).

7 Quoted in the *New York Times*, February 25, 2003, page D4.

8 John Gabarro and John Kotter, "Managing Your Boss," *Harvard Business Review*, May/June, 1993.

9 These expectations are expressed through the core values. See Chapter 1.

Practice #4: Manage Decisions Well

1 When polled, most leaders say they are comfortable with 75 percent certainty that a given decision will achieve the goal.

2 The GROW model was initially developed by John Whitmore in his book *Coaching for Performance* (Boston: Nicholas Brealey, 1996).

3 Finding out your style is free. Go to www.gostraighttalk.com.

4 David Dunning and Justin Kruger, "Unskilled and Unaware of It: How Difficulties in Recognizing One's Own Incompetence Lead to Inflated Self Assessments," *Journal of Personality and Social Psychology*, June 10, 1999.

Practice #5: Start With Yourself

1 Warren Bennis, *Managing People Is Like Herding Cats* (Utah: Executive Excellence Publishing, 1999).

2 Joseph Singer, *The Edges of the Field: Lessons on the Obligations of Ownership* (Boston, MA: Beacon Press, 2000).

3 Rushworth Kidder, *How Good People Make Tough Choices* (New York: Harper Collins/Quill, 2003).

4 Lance Secretan, as quoted in *Industry Week*, October 12, 1998. Secretan is author of, among others, *Reclaiming Higher Ground: Creating Organizations That Inspire the Soul* (Canada: CDG Books, 1997).

5 Jamba Juice, Investor Relations, http://ir.jambajuice.com/phoenix.zhtml?c=192409&p=irol-irhome.

6 IMDB biography for Richard Branson, http://www.imdb.com/name/nm0105232/bio.

7   Brent Schlender, "How Big Can Apple Get," *Fortune*, February 21, 2005.
8   "The Most Admired Leaders Challenge Stereotypes, But Feel They Are Unexceptional," *Washington CEO*, 1997.
9   From Enron's 1998 Annual Report, excerpted from: Bethany McLean and Peter Elkin, *The Smartest Guys in the Room: The Amazing Rise and Scandalous Fall of Enron* (New York: Penguin Group, 2003).
10 Virginia Satir, *The New Peoplemaking* (Palo Alto: Science & Behavior Books, 1988).
11 *Straight Talk: Turning Communication Upside Down for Strategic Results*. Available online at all major booksellers and at our website: www.LeadingResources.com.
12 Daniel Goleman, "Leadership Gets Results," *Harvard Business Review*, March/April, 2000.
13 You can go to www.gostraighttalk.com to learn your communication style. The survey is free, fast, and accurate.

Create Spark
Practice #6: Accelerate the Pace of Change

1   "The Little Ideas That Could," *New York Times*, June 14, 1998.
2   Eric Hoffer, *Reflections on the Human Condition* (New Jersey: Hopewell Publications, 2006).
3   Our Straight Talk® survey of communication styles can be a useful tool in gathering a good mix of styles. The survey and results are free. Visit www.gostraighttalk.com.

Practice #7: Stimulate Creative Flow

1   Mihaly Csikszentmihalyi, *Flow: The Psychology of Optimal Experience* (New York: Harper & Row, 1990).
2   University of Chicago's General Social Survey (a survey of Americans conducted since 1972). More information can be found at http://www.norc.org/Research/Projects/Pages/general-social-survey.aspx.
3   George Patton, *War as I Knew It* (Boston: Houghton Mifflin Harcourt, 1995).
4   Ellen Langer and Deborah Heffernan, "Mindful Managing: Confident but Uncertain Managers," Harvard University, Department of Psychology, 1988.

Practice #8: Spread Systems Thinking

1   The book *We Don't Make Widgets* is a good source of additional insight into systems of work: Ken Miller, *We Don't Make Widgets* (Washington, DC: Governing Books, 2013).

Practice #9: Multiply the Communication

1   "Lawrence Rawl, 76; Exxon Chief at Time of Alaskan Oil Spill Disaster," *Los Angeles Times*, February 15, 2005.
2   Phil Jackson and Hugh Delehanty, *Sacred Hoops: Spiritual Lessons of a Hardwood Warrior* (New York: Hyperion, 1995).

Practice #10: Ask Powerful Questions

1   John C. Maxwell, *The 21 Indispensable Qualities of a Leader: Follow Them and People Will Follow You* (Nashville: Thomas Nelson, 2007).

INDEX

ABOUT THE AUTHOR

Eric Douglas is a senior partner and founder of Leading Resources Inc., a consulting firm that focuses on developing high-performing organizations. For more than twenty years, Eric has successfully helped a wide array of government agencies, nonprofit organizations, and corporations achieve breakthroughs in performance.

An honors graduate of Harvard University, Eric started his career as a newspaper reporter and editor at the San Francisco Chronicle. He began consulting in the 1990s, where he discovered his true passion—"changing the world from the inside out, rather than from the outside looking in."

Eric's expertise is in helping leaders with strategy, governance, and performance management. His work as a leadership coach and consultant has been recognized by the Institute of Management Consultants. He also devotes considerable time to charitable and community projects. He is married and has four children. In whatever time he has left over, he enjoys songwriting, sailing, and travel.

Find more articles by Eric at www.LeadingResources.com.